LEGENDS & LORE

YEAR OF THE DRAGON

DEDICATED TO DEE AND GARETH; AND TEYA, DAUGHTER OF THE DRAGON

龍年

LEGENDS & LORE

FRIEDMAN/FAIRFAX
PUBLISHERS

A FRIEDMAN/FAIRFAX BOOK

Please visit our website: www.metrobooks.com

This edition published by the Michael Friedman Publishing Group
by arrangement with Pavilion Books
2003 Friedman/Fairfax Publishers

ISBN 1 58663 930 7

First published in Great Britain in 2000 by
PAVILION BOOKS
A member of Chrysalis Books plc

64 Brewery Road, London, N7 9NT

Distributed by Sterling Publishing Company, Inc.
387 Park Avenue South
New York, NY 10016

Distributed in Australia by
Capricorn Link (Australia) Pty, Ltd.
P.O. Box 704, Windsor, NSW 2756 Australia

Text © 2002 Nigel Suckling
Illustrations © 2002 Wayne Anderson
Design and layout © Pavilion Books Ltd.
All calligraphy by Lifen Zhang

Set in Bernhard Modern

Printed and bound by Imago, China

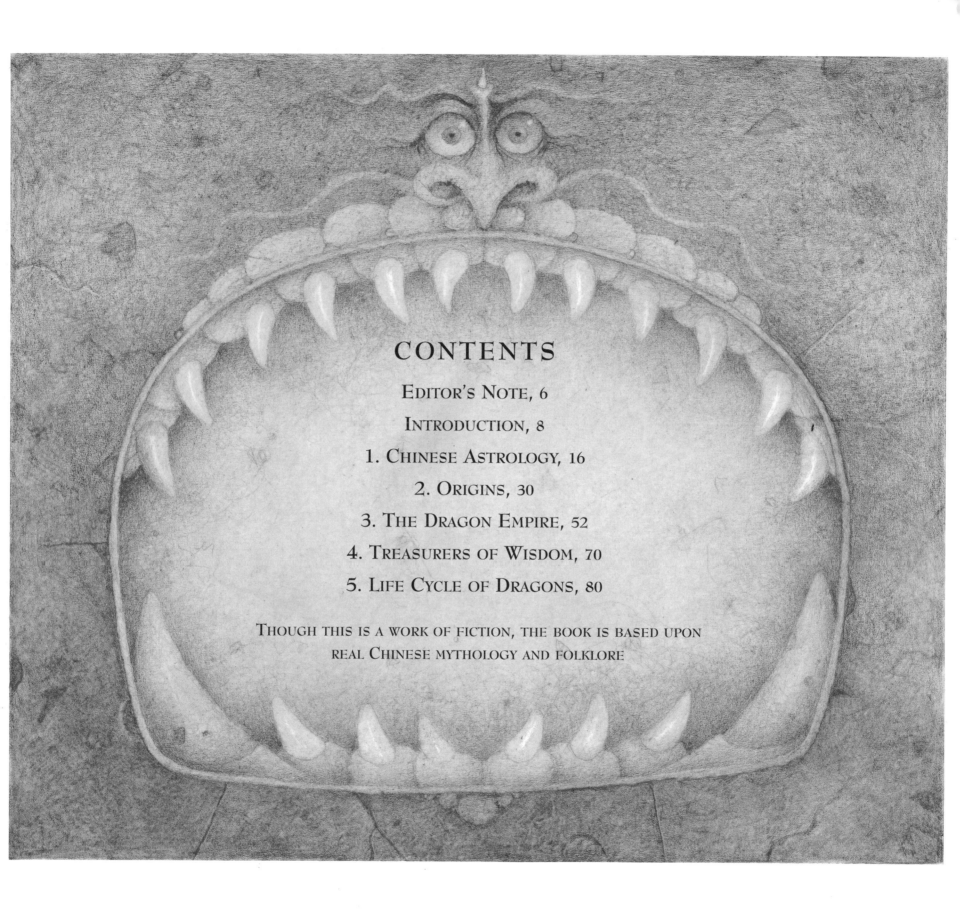

CONTENTS

THOUGH THIS IS A WORK OF FICTION, THE BOOK IS BASED UPON
REAL CHINESE MYTHOLOGY AND FOLKLORE

EDITOR'S NOTE

THE CHANCE DISCOVERY, IN A SUFFOLK AUCTION IN 1998, OF A JOURNAL WRITTEN BY AN ENGLISH TRAVELLER IN CHINA – AND PUBLISHED HERE FOR THE FIRST TIME – WAS ONE OF THOSE FINDS THAT ARE AT ONCE DELIGHTFUL, UNEXPECTED AND, ULTIMATELY, HIGHLY MYSTERIOUS.

HOW had it ended up in a bargain job lot of household effects? Who was the author? Was he – or she (or maybe there was more than one writer?) – also the illustrator? Were they travelling around China on business, or could they possibly have been missionaries? We have very little idea. Indeed, it's only because of a passing reference in the text that we can even deduce that it was written in the late eighteenth century.

Throughout his or her journal the author speaks of 'we' – but this could just be modesty. We can only make intelligent guesses about the author's personality from the kinds of things he or she has chosen to describe, the anecdotes that have caught his or her interest.

Particularly striking is an apparent lack of cultural bias which is very unusual for the time – a complete contrast, for

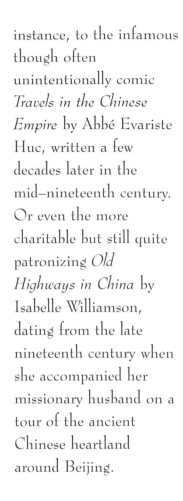

instance, to the infamous though often unintentionally comic *Travels in the Chinese Empire* by Abbé Evariste Huc, written a few decades later in the mid–nineteenth century. Or even the more charitable but still quite patronizing *Old Highways in China* by Isabelle Williamson, dating from the late nineteenth century when she accompanied her missionary husband on a tour of the ancient Chinese heartland around Beijing.

There are suggestions that the journal was meant to be expanded or form part of some larger work. The author assumes we know who he, she or they are and why they are in China; but it hardly matters that we don't. What this record offers is a unique insight into the beliefs, and in a sense the reality, of dragons in China a couple of centuries ago, just before the onset of the great cultural upheavals which are still unfolding.

Much of its dragon lore has surfaced elsewhere through being preserved in collections of folktales and classics of literature such as *The Wonders by Mountain and Sea* and *The Songs of Qu,* which are almost as accessible to us in modern translation as to our bibliophile traveller in China two centuries ago. But much also seems to have been gathered at first hand in far-flung corners of the Chinese Empire. A few of the journal's claims clash with current popular notions about Chinese dragons, but mostly they just add to what we already know.

WE have tidied up the text slightly to make it more palatable to modern readers. The author's often rather flowery style of writing has had to be pruned, quite drastically in places, but this was simply a matter of dropping extraneous words and phrases here and there. Nothing significant was added, so what you are about to read is pretty much exactly what he (or she) was trying to say — except without the digressions. We have also cleaned up the often wildly erratic spelling of Chinese words in the original. To preserve the flavour, certain names such as Peking and Genghis Khan have been kept in the familiar form the author employs, but otherwise we have used modern Pin Yin wherever possible.

INTRODUCTION

ALMOST THE FIRST THING ONE NOTICES IN CHINA IS THE UBIQUITY OF THE DRAGON. IT PERMEATES VERY NEARLY EVERY ASPECT OF CHINESE CULTURE.

ALL major feasts and celebrations feature dragons and they are portrayed on every side in both town and country – on ships, bridges and roof gables, embroidered on silk, glazed into ceramics and carved into wood and stone. Particularly so in Peking where we had the good fortune to stay on several occasions in our travels.

Here one finds the five-toed golden dragon everywhere, for it is the emblem of the Emperor. All his immediate retinue have it embroidered somewhere or other on their dress, and those who presume to wear it without authorization generally have their heads removed from their shoulders with little ceremony. Such is the power of the Emperor's dragon that envoys or messengers wearing it can travel unmolested from one end of the Celestial Empire to another, and meet every possible hospitality along the way at the expense of the local mandarins. Lesser officials must make do instead with lesser dragons with four or three toes and meet with correspondingly less respect.

The Emperor is surrounded by images of the dragon. He sits on a Dragon Throne, sleeps in a Dragon Bed and has the 'true' five-toed dragon embroidered onto his official robes and the banners that

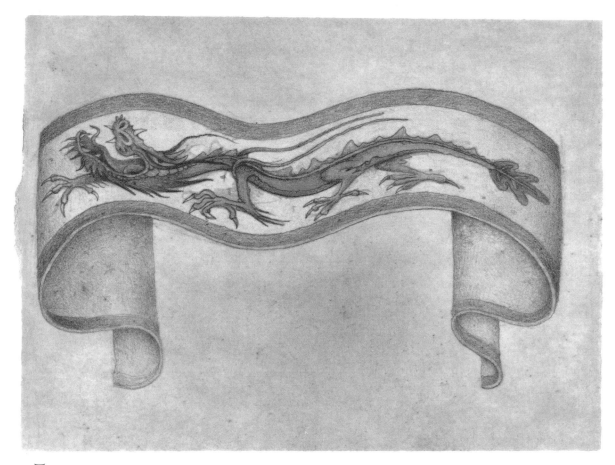

THE FOUR-TOED DRAGON ON A BANNER OR COSTUME DENOTES A PRINCE OF THE REALM. THREE-TOED DRAGONS SIGNIFY DUKES AND CERTAIN HIGH-RANKING GOVERNMENT MINISTERS. BANNERS WERE FIRST MADE POPULAR IN CHINA, THEY SAY, BY GHENGHIS KHAN.

accompany him everywhere. A dragon (or a pair of dragons playing with a pearl) is the seal on the edicts he issues on golden paper. All books authorized or commissioned by the Emperor also bear his dragon seal and, again, anyone who abuses it meets with swift retribution.

The Emperor also has an elaborate ceremonial barge built in the likeness of a dragon which he sails on the lakes of the Garden of Perfect Brightness (Yuan Ming Yuan) near Peking, a wonderland where treasures, buildings and curiosities have been gathered from all corners of his realm. We call it China, but the

have had dragon blood in their veins, and even to have been able to turn into dragons at will. Even Yu, founder of the historical Xia dynasty in about 2,000 BC, is said to have been born as a dragon and have supernatural powers. His more fully human successors are supposed still to have had a dragonish cast to their countenances, and to be called 'dragon-face' is considered a great compliment in China to this day. The Chinese say their current Emperor's lineage can be traced directly back to those distant founders of the state, so his eyes are called 'dragon's eyes' and his beard is a 'dragon beard'. In a very real sense the Emperor is seen as the incarnation on earth of the spirit of his people, which is a celestial dragon.

Chinese themselves prefer simply the Middle Kingdom, Zhongguo, meaning that it exists halfway between Heaven and the underworld. The name China that we use derives from the Qin (Chin) dynasty who first united the country, more or less as we know it today, in the third century BC, expanding from their homeland around the Yellow River in the north.

ONE reason for the profusion of dragons around the Emperor is that his earliest legendary forerunners such, as Huangdi and Shun, are claimed to

JAPANESE NETSUKE
UNICORN (LEFT)
AND DRAGON.

IN a diluted sense the entire people of China believe they share this inheritance and will often proudly claim to visiting foreigners such as ourselves that they are all 'Long de Chuanren' – Descendants of the Dragon. In Japan they apparently hold very similar beliefs and the Japanese Emperor also traces his lineage back to a dragon, the princess Fruitful Jewel, daughter of the Dragon King of the Eastern Ocean.

The more sophisticated elements in Chinese society, particularly in Peking, no longer seriously believe in dragons as a physical species. They will tell you that they died out long ago and have become purely spiritual beings, gods even. Some even question whether they ever did exist as they appear in the legends, but in the countryside and farther reaches of the Empire there is no such detachment. There they firmly believe that when the earth shakes it is because treasure-guarding dragons are stirring below ground. Rivers flood when they are restless beneath the waves. When thunderstorms rage it is due to the mating or battle of dragons in the sky, real Leviathans of flesh and blood who at any moment might fall and flatten the village below. One even hears tales of this happening not just long ago in legend, but today.

EMPEROR QIANLONG (1736-95)

On our travels we met witnesses in several different parts of the country who swore to having lost family, friends and neighbours in such catastrophes. Despite these occasional disasters, people do not consider dragons evil. There are exceptions which we will come to later, but on the whole it is quite the opposite. Dragons in China are revered as basically wise and gracious divine beings, great benefactors of humanity because they are masters of the weather. There are gods of weather with human form, but they take second place to dragons. It is dragons who are believed to dispense the fertilizing rains so essential for the annual crop. Natural disasters are attributed to their carelessness, neglect or righteous anger; so offerings to dragons are designed more to win their attention and favour than to appease any natural inborn malice.

These sacrifices, mostly appealing for the right measure of rain, are made at countless waterside temples in China. Every well, stream, river and lake has its temple, be it ever so small, where on the first and fifteenth day of the month (the new and full moons) the owner, or the people living

nearby, come to make offerings to the dragon they sincerely believe to dwell in the water.

An old Chinaman in an opium den in Canton (now called Guangzhou) once told us a cautionary tale when we suggested to him that perhaps dragons were purely mythical or imaginary creatures. He told us that not long ago the Emperor Qianlong had reached a similar conclusion and determined to put the matter to the test. Accordingly he visited the famous Black Dragon Pool (Hei Longtan, generally reserved for the Empress), a little to the west of Peking, where offerings have been made to the resident dragon since time immemorial. Going to the water's edge at the temple there, surrounded by his courtiers, he burned incense in the customary manner and cast offerings into the pool, calling all the while for the dragon to show himself. All that surfaced among the lilies was a little water-lizard. The Emperor laughed aloud and cried: 'Is this the mighty dragon to whom we make so many rich offerings? Why he's lucky not to have been eaten by the carp!'

The lizard raised one tiny foot out of the water, and this foot grew suddenly larger and larger until it hung like a canopy over the pool. Then it grew larger still until it covered the whole sky and its claws threatened to topple distant mountains. The Emperor fell to his knees and begged the dragon to return to its former size, promising anything it wished in return. And when Qianlong had been suitably humbled, the dragon relented and resumed its customary abode in the depths of the lake.

However, when we repeated this story to a friend in Peking he only laughed and said it was a fairytale because he had served the Emperor Qianlong himself as a junior clerk, and would certainly have heard if anything like it had actually happened.

So within China there exists a wide spectrum of belief concerning dragons, ranging from outright scepticism to complete and unquestioning faith, but all unite happily for the great dragon festivals which are such a feature of the Chinese calendar; and all accept the dragon as the single most telling embodiment or symbol of the Chinese spirit.

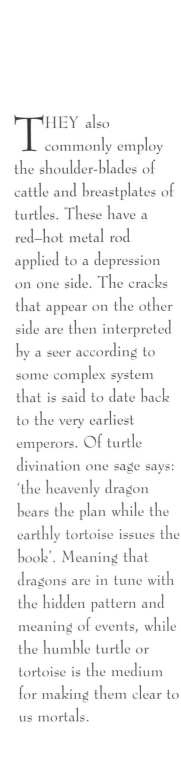

CHINESE ASTROLOGY

THE CHINESE HAVE COUNTLESS WAYS OF SEEKING TO DIVINE THE FUTURE AND EVEN TODAY THE HIGHEST DECISIONS OF STATE ARE TAKEN ONLY AFTER CONSULTING SOME ORACLE OR OTHER. THE MOST POPULAR INVOLVE THE USE OF YARROW STALKS OR COINS IN CONJUNCTION WITH AN ANCIENT MANUAL OF WISDOM SAID TO HAVE BEEN WRITTEN IN PART BY CONFUCIUS, BUT BASED ON OTHER WRITINGS THAT WERE ANCIENT EVEN IN HIS DAY (SIXTH CENTURY BC).

THEY also commonly employ the shoulder-blades of cattle and breastplates of turtles. These have a red–hot metal rod applied to a depression on one side. The cracks that appear on the other side are then interpreted by a seer according to some complex system that is said to date back to the very earliest emperors. Of turtle divination one sage says: 'the heavenly dragon bears the plan while the earthly tortoise issues the book'. Meaning that dragons are in tune with the hidden pattern and meaning of events, while the humble turtle or tortoise is the medium for making them clear to us mortals.

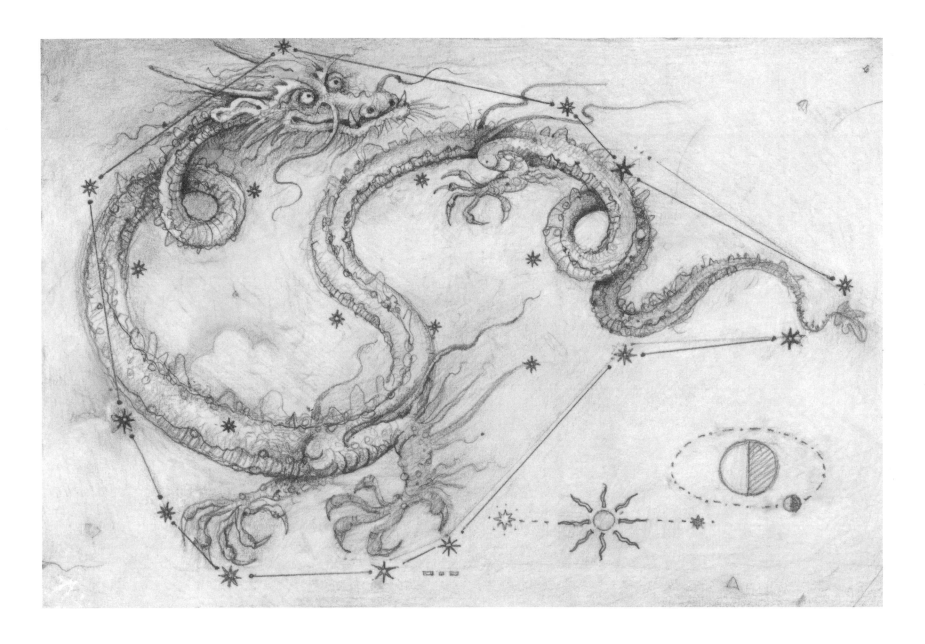

The Chinese also have their own system of astrology which we found the easiest of these methods to understand, although it is totally different to European astrology. The initial likeness between their zodiac and ours is completely misleading. They look similar because both are commonly shown as wheels divided into twelve segments, each containing an astrological sign. But whereas in Western astrology the wheel represents the solar year divided into twelve months, in China each segment is itself a year carrying the symbol of an animal. Everyone born in that year has the same dominating birth sign and will be a rat, an ox, a dragon, or whichever animal is appointed to rule over the year.

GIVEN the diversity of human nature and fortune this may seem a very broad brush with which to paint, although it makes the system commendably simple for an outsider to grasp; but Chinese astrology is in practice far more subtle and complex than it first appears. What practitioners say is that yes, indeed, everyone born in a particular year will have their life indelibly stamped with the animal character of that year, but they also have individual destinies determined by the month, day and hour of their birth. So it is quite possible within the terms of Chinese astrology for an individual to be born in the luckiest of years and yet enjoy the most miserable of existences (and vice versa), owing to other factors linked with their moment of birth.

The most curious thing to our eyes about the Chinese zodiac is that, of the twelve signs, only one – the dragon – is what we would consider a mythical beast. The rest are all creatures familiar to every peasant: the Ox, the Rooster, the Boar and so on. They are totem beasts with whose patterns of behaviour it is easy enough to relate. Some might shrink from being dubbed with the sign of the Rat or Pig, but the Chinese do not see it like that at all. Both these creatures, they say, have many admirable traits. Their despised qualities are merely their negative aspects, which all the other signs equally possess. Each totem beast has a good and bad side.

The presence of the dragon in the zodiac shows how firmly the Chinese believe in this beast. To most of them the dragon is as real as the other animals. It is unique only in being the one creature of their zodiac credited with supernatural powers. So the Year of the Dragon, which recurs every twelve years, is considered particularly lucky and children born in that year are believed to be blessed with health, wealth and a long life. It is also a good year for beginning new undertakings for everyone, whatever their birth sign. The Year of the Hare, by contrast, is generally calm and peaceful because the hare has a strong link with the moon through the divine Hare that dwells there with moon goddess Chang'e. Earthly hares show this by having a gestation period of exactly one lunar month.

BUDDHA DEPARTING
FROM THIS WORLD.

THE animals of the Chinese zodiac are, in order of appearance: Rat, Ox, Tiger, Hare, Dragon, Snake, Horse, Sheep, Monkey, Rooster, Dog and Pig. One tradition has it that these are the twelve beasts who came to bid farewell to the Buddha upon his departure from this world, and their reward was to be placed in the zodiac. But those less influenced by Buddhism have other tales.

The most popular we heard of was that the Supreme Being, the Yellow Emperor of Heaven, Huangdi, decided one day that humans needed some kind of compass to guide them through the invisible maze of life's undertakings. So he decided to create the zodiac. To decide upon the symbols he announced to all the animals of the world that there would be a race, and the first twelve beasts to cross the finishing line would be chosen to stand forever as signs of human character and destiny.

On the eve of the great race all the beasts went to sleep early to be fresh for the dawn start. But in the night Ox suddenly awoke and thought: 'I am so slow that if I am to have any chance at all of being among the twelve I had better start now.' So he did, but as he passed among the other sleeping animals he woke Rat, who guessed his plan and thought: 'I am so small that no matter how hard I run even Ox will beat me at this rate.' So he scurried up a tree and dropped so lightly on to Ox's back as he passed below that he did not notice.

At dawn the other animals awoke (all except Dragon who overslept), found that Ox and Rat had gone and raced off after them as fast as they could, but no matter how fast they ran they could not catch up. When the finishing line came into view they all saw Ox comfortably ahead of them and about to cross the line. Ox paused to look back and was pleased to see how well his plan had worked. But as he paused, Rat leaped off his back and raced across the line. Which is why Rat comes first in the zodiac, followed by Ox and then all the rest of the twelve.

We heard many variations of this tale, but what they all share is the idea of Rat achieving first place by riding upon Ox's back. It is also often said that the reason for the enmity between cats and rats is because Rat had promised to awaken Cat for the race and she missed her place in the zodiac by oversleeping.

CHINESE ZODIAC IN RELATION TO THE WESTERN CALENDAR.
(THE DATES HAVE BEEN AMENDED TO SUIT OUR CURRENT CALENDER)

BY A CURIOUS COINCIDENCE, THE CHINESE SIGNS OF THE ZODIAC, AS APPLIED TO THE SOLAR YEAR, CORRESPOND ALMOST EXACTLY WITH THE DATES THAT DEFINE THE WESTERN ZODIAC. SO IF YOU KNOW YOUR WESTERN BIRTH SIGN, IT ALSO TELLS YOU THE CHINESE ONE FOR YOUR DATE OF BIRTH, THOUGH THE CHINESE CONSIDER THIS LESS IMPORTANT THAN YOUR YEAR SIGN.

THE SAME ELEMENT APPEARS ON CONSECUTIVE YEARS IN THE YEAR CHART OPPOSITE. THE ELEMENT IN THE FIRST YEAR IS YANG, THE SECOND YIN. (SEE CHAPTER 4 PAGE 79)

WHEN APPLIED TO THE HOURS OF THE DAY, (SEE CHART BELOW) EACH CHINESE SIGN COVERS TWO HOURS, THE FIRST BEING YANG, THE SECOND YIN.

			YANG	YIN
Rat	Sagittarius	Rat	11pm – 12	12 – 1am
Ox	Capricorn	Ox	1am – 2am	2am – 3am
Tiger	Aquarius	Tiger	3am – 4am	4am – 5am
Hare	Pisces	Hare	5am – 6am	6am – 7am
Dragon	Aries	Dragon	7am – 8am	8am – 9am
Snake	Taurus	Snake	9am – 10am	10am – 11am
Horse	Gemini	Horse	11am – 12	12 – 1pm
Sheep	Cancer	Sheep	1pm – 2pm	2pm – 3pm
Monkey	Leo	Monkey	3pm – 4pm	4pm – 5pm
Rooster	Virgo	Rooster	5pm – 6pm	6pm – 7pm
Dog	Libra	Dog	7pm – 8pm	8pm – 9pm
Pig	Scorpio	Pig	9pm – 10pm	10pm – 11pm

RAT	OX	TIGER	HARE	DRAGON	SNAKE	HORSE	SHEEP	MONKEY	ROOSTER	DOG	PIG
					Year:	1930	1931	1932	1933	1934	1935
					Chinese New Year begins on:	30 Jan	17 Feb	6 Feb	26 Jan	14 Feb	4 Feb
					Element associated with that year:	Metal	Metal	Water	Water	Wood	Wood
1936	1937	1938	1939	1940	1941	1942	1943	1944	1945	1946	1947
24 Jan	11 Feb	31 Jan	19 Feb	8 Feb	27 Jan	15 Feb	5 Feb	25 Jan	13 Feb	2 Feb	22 Jan
Fire	Fire	Earth	Earth	Metal	Metal	Water	Water	Wood	Wood	Fire	Fire
1948	1949	1950	1951	1952	1953	1954	1955	1956	1957	1958	1959
8 Feb	29 Jan	17 Feb	6 Feb	27 Jan	14 Feb	3 Feb	24 Jan	12 Feb	31 Jan	18 Feb	8 Feb
Earth	Earth	Metal	Metal	Water	Water	Wood	Wood	Fire	Fire	Earth	Earth
1960	1961	1962	1963	1964	1965	1966	1967	1968	1969	1970	1971
28 Jan	15 Feb	5 Feb	25 Jan	13 Feb	2 Feb	21 Jan	9 Feb	30 Jan	17 Feb	6 Feb	27 Jan
Metal	Metal	Water	Water	Wood	Wood	Fire	Fire	Earth	Earth	Metal	Metal
1972	1973	1974	1975	1976	1977	1978	1979	1980	1981	1982	1983
16 Feb	3 Feb	23 Jan	11 Feb	31 Jan	18 Feb	7 Feb	28 Jan	16 Feb	5 Feb	25 Jan	13 Feb
Water	Water	Wood	Wood	Fire	Fire	Earth	Earth	Metal	Metal	Water	Water
1984	1985	1986	1987	1988	1989	1990	1991	1992	1993	1994	1995
2 Feb	20 Feb	9 Feb	29 Jan	17 Feb	6 Feb	27 Jan	15 Feb	4 Feb	23 Jan	10 Feb	31 Jan
Wood	Wood	Fire	Fire	Earth	Earth	Metal	Metal	Water	Water	Wood	Wood
1996	1997	1998	1999	2000	2001	2002	2003	2004	2005	2006	2007
19 Feb	8 Feb	28 Jan	16 Feb	5 Feb	24 Jan	12 Feb	1 Feb	22 Jan	9 Feb	29 Jan	18 Feb
Fire	Fire	Earth	Earth	Metal	Metal	Water	Water	Wood	Wood	Fire	Fire
2008	2009	2010									
7 Feb	26 Jan	14 Feb									
Earth	Earth	Metal									

THE FOLLOWING, IN BRIEF, IS WHAT THE CHINESE SAY OF THE
QUALITIES OF THE DIFFERENT ASTROLOGICAL SIGNS:

RAT
POSITIVE QUALITIES

Quick-wittedness,
adaptability, charm,
sociability and intelligence;
gifted in mathematics, music
and business

OX
POSITIVE QUALITIES

Reliability, perseverance,
loyalty, thoroughness; oxen
make good partners but are
rarely leaders in their
own right

TIGER
POSITIVE QUALITIES

Ambition, charisma,
confidence, courage,
dedication; tigers make good
leaders and warriors

HARE
POSITIVE QUALITIES

Sociability, diplomacy,
sincerity, empathy, modesty,
trustworthiness; hares make
good healers, herbalists,
diplomats, gardeners and
domestic partners

RAT
NEGATIVE QUALITIES

Slyness, inconstancy,
promiscuity, carelessness

OX
NEGATIVE QUALITIES

Stubbornness, lack of
charisma, misanthropy

TIGER
NEGATIVE QUALITIES

Aggression, ruthlessness,
indifference to others'
opinions

HARE
NEGATIVE QUALITIES

Over-cautiousness,
insecurity, moodiness,
shrewishness, complaining

DRAGON
POSITIVE QUALITIES

Flamboyance, idealism, perfectionism, charisma, imagination, flexibility, showmanship, luck and generosity; dragons make good political and religious leaders, actors and artists

SNAKE
POSITIVE QUALITIES

Decisiveness, intelligence, intuitiveness, elegance, attention to detail; snakes make good philosophers, organizers and writers

HORSE
POSITIVE QUALITIES

Adventurousness, courage, charisma, ambition, sociability, intelligence, loyalty; horses make great explorers, travelling merchants, generals

SHEEP
POSITIVE QUALITIES

Elegance, charm, sensitivity, taste, warmth, loyalty; sheep make better craftsmen than artists

DRAGON
NEGATIVE QUALITIES

Lack of realism, temper when plans go wrong, laziness

SNAKE
NEGATIVE QUALITIES

Miserliness, deviousness, manipulativeness

HORSE
NEGATIVE QUALITIES

Restlessness, impatience, recklessness, self-centredness

SHEEP
NEGATIVE QUALITIES

Indecisiveness, caution, subservience, limited in outlook

MONKEY
POSITIVE QUALITIES

Liveliness, wit, curiosity, intelligence, charm, luck; monkeys can adapt to almost any occupation but need the guiding hand of a master to achieve anything of worth

ROOSTER
POSITIVE QUALITIES

Energy, intelligence, flexibility, flamboyance, outspokenness; roosters are almost as adaptable as monkeys in their careers but more reliable

DOG
POSITIVE QUALITIES

Loyalty, intelligence, energy, courage, sociability; dogs are invaluable community members without necessarily wanting to be leaders

PIG
POSITIVE QUALITIES

Sincerity, tolerance, sociability, cheerfulness, determination, optimism, honour, contentment; like the Dog, the Pig is more concerned with domestic and local community matters than larger issues

MONKEY
NEGATIVE QUALITIES

Frivolousness, arrogance, mischievousness, unreliability

ROOSTER
NEGATIVE QUALITIES

Vanity, aggressiveness, abrasiveness, impatience with others

DOG
NEGATIVE QUALITIES

Aggression, unpredictability, narrowness, over-conservatism

PIG
NEGATIVE QUALITIES

Laziness, gluttony, indifference to the larger issues

These are the birth signs of Chinese astrology but practitioners will tell you that no individual is likely to match the characteristics of any sign closely unless the month, hour and even minute of their birth happens to coincide with the prevailing sign for the year. If, for example, one happens to be born in the Hour of the Sheep, the Month of the Pig and the Year of the Dragon, then the characteristics of all those signs will interact in a complex way and none will predominate. Whereas if the minute, hour, month and year of one's birth all fall within the sign of the Ox, then one should display that sign's qualities in abundance.

THERE are also other factors which rapidly complicate the picture. The signs recur every twelve years, but each time they do they come under the influence of a different one of the Five Sacred Elements, which alters their influence upon those born under the sign. This means that it is in fact sixty years before any sign fully returns; and this sixty-year cycle is the basis of all Chinese chronology. It is said that their oldest book is an almanac known as Red and Black, detailing the progression of the signs and elements from the present right back to the very day Huangdi created the zodiac in the year 2256 BC.

In addition there is the operation of the Yin-Yang duality at the heart of all creation. This means that all factors can manifest in either active or passive modes. All this rapidly creates a complex system that would require a book in itself to do it justice. But in our brief study we were impressed by the subtlety of Chinese astrology and felt that is was just as possible to sketch a character in its terms as in those of Western astrology. Of course, whether or not one believes the moment of one's birth has any bearing at all on one's character and fortunes is a matter of personal taste. Our own minds remain open, possibly even sceptical on this point; but we were, nonetheless, most impressed by the seeming accuracy of our portraits as drawn by Chinese astrologers, as far as the character profile goes anyway. With our predicted fortunes we shall just have to wait and see. Chinese astrology is admirably direct and down to earth in its predictions. They generally concern health, wealth and happiness, in that order.

However, we were less interested in whether the Chinese (or any) form of astrology actually works, than in what it had to say about the Chinese view of human nature, as reflected through their zodiac totems. In particular we wanted to know what astrologers had to say about the dragon, because we reasoned that this would give the clearest possible insight into Chinese opinion about the nature of the beast.

Here is what we read in one astrology manual:

The Dragon is the sign of Power and Magnificence. When he flies abroad wreathed in smoke and fire he can be seen from 100,000 paces. The people flock to his call and the mighty tremble in their palaces for fear of his wrath. He is the guardian of wealth and wears it like a shining armour. When the Dragon mounts to heaven, the rains come and prosperity follows. The Dragon is generous and forgiving. His rage is as lightning, but it soon passes. When the Dragon acts in accord with the Way nothing can withstand him. When the Dragon is in conflict with the Way disaster swiftly follows. He falls to the ground and becomes a succulent dinner for the myriad hungry people. The Dragon is magnificent but can be deaf to wise counsel. The Dragon prefers battle to diplomacy.

A human born under the sign of the Dragon during a storm will have a tempestuous life. If the sea and sky are calm, then so will be their lives. The Dragon is persevering, honest and a loyal champion. The Dragon mates particularly well with the Monkey, Rat and Snake. With the Ox his relationship will be troubled and with the Dog miserable.

The Dragon who is in a lowly position does well not to boast of what he will achieve but cling to his true path. In time his worth will be recognized and rewarded by the multitude. The lowly Dragon who is impatient to fly meets only with opposition and ridicule. If he bides his time till his horns are grown, then he will rise swift and surely to Heaven and be revered by the people.

This was the clearest summation we could find of the supposed qualities of the dragon sign and it well expresses the imperial nature of the beast. Dragons are meant to rule and be admired for their magnificence but it is interesting how the dangers of

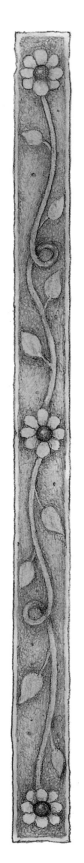

such a condition are clearly indicated. This is something we found at every turn in Chinese astrology, and their philosophy generally for that matter. In their feudal system rulers have immense power, but they are surrounded by advice from all sides on the correct and wise exercise of that power, and the perils of exceeding its limits. Tales of both Emperors and dragons that have fallen from grace are told and retold with relish as a veiled warning perhaps from the populace to their rulers that their grasp on the reins of earthly power is not all that counts.

'IN ADDITION THERE IS THE OPERATION OF THE YIN-YANG DUALITY AT THE HEART OF ALL CREATION.'

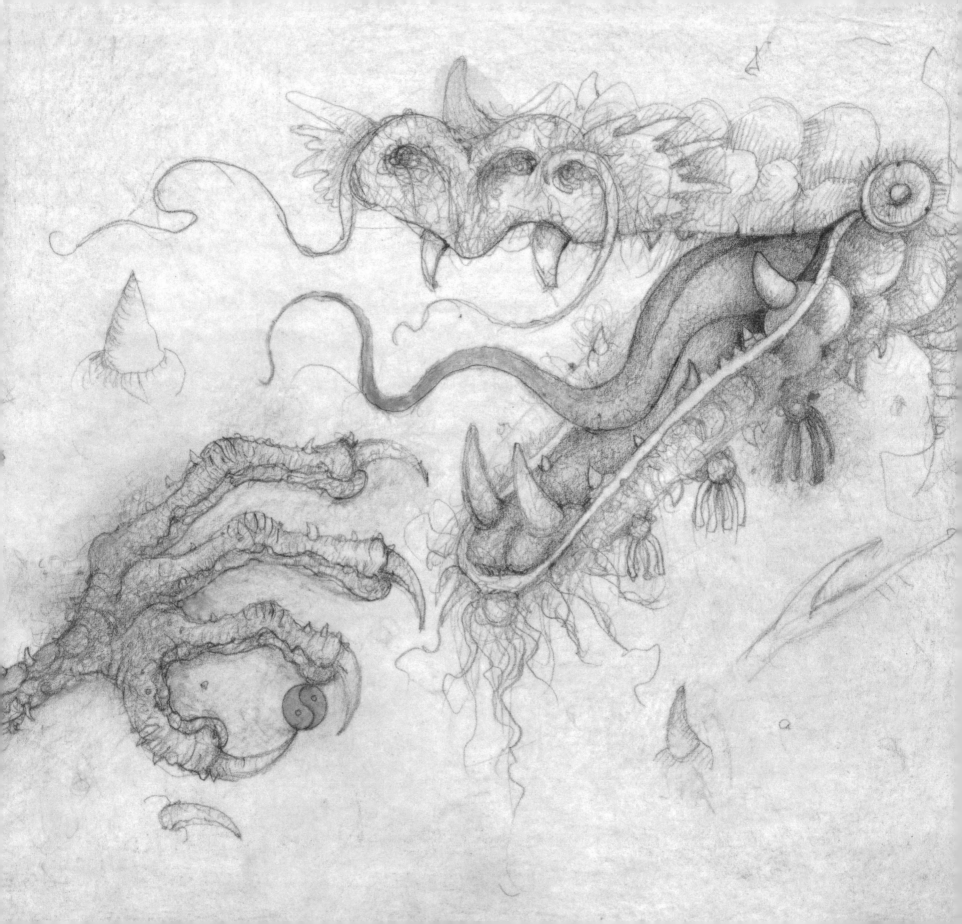

ORIGINS

THE CHINESE SAY THAT IN THE VERY BEGINNING NOTHING EXISTED BUT FORMLESS CHAOS. THEN SOME OF THE MATTER OF THIS CHAOS COLLECTED TO FORM A COSMIC EGG, IN WHICH THE OPPOSED PRINCIPLES OF YIN AND YANG WERE PERFECTLY BALANCED. FOR AN AGE THE EGG HUNG IN THE VOID, THEN IT WAS QUICKENED, NO ONE IS SURE HOW, AND WITHIN IT TOOK THE FORM OF PANGU, THE FIRST MAN. HE IS GENERALLY PORTRAYED AS A HAIRY PRIMITIVE GIANT WITH AN ENORMOUS CLUB, MUCH LIKE OUR OWN HERCULES. PANGU SLOWLY GREW TILL HE FILLED THE EGG. THEN HE STIRRED AND WOKE AND CHAFED AT HIS CONFINEMENT.

HE reached out and his hand closed around an axe. Impatiently he struck out with it and burst free. Then he separated the Yin from the Yang and fashioned from them the earth and sky, which he forced apart by standing between them as he grew at a rate of ten feet a day.

THE PHOENIX IS OFTEN SEEN AS THE FEMALE COUNTERPART OF THE ESSENTIALLY MALE DRAGON. PICTURES SHOWING A DRAGON AND PHOENIX TOGETHER SYMBOLIZE THE IDEAL MARRIAGE AND ARE OFTEN GIVEN AT WEDDINGS. ON THE OTHER HAND THERE ARE ALSO SAID TO BE FEMALE DRAGONS AND MALE PHOENIXES WHO PAIR IN THE NORMAL WAY.

THE CHINESE UNICORN OR QI LIN IS SAID TO APPEAR AT THE START AND END OF A GOOD EMPEROR'S REIGN, AND THE ANCIENT ANNALS OFTEN RECORD SUCH EVENTS. CONFUCIUS' BIRTH AND DEATH ARE ALSO SAID TO HAVE BEEN HERALDED BY UNICORN SIGHTINGS. HE IS OFTEN CALLED THE 'KING WITHOUT A CROWN' BECAUSE, DESPITE HIS VAST INFLUENCE ON CHINESE THOUGHT AND GOVERNMENT, HE HELD NO SIGNIFICANT RANK DURING HIS LIFETIME.

THE TURTLE (OR TORTOISE, THE CHINESE DO NOT DISTINGUISH BETWEEN THEM) IS THE MOST EARTHBOUND OF THE FOUR MOST FORTUNATE BEASTS, WHICH IS WHY THE LEGS OF A GIANT TURTLE ARE SAID TO HAVE BEEN CHOSEN TO SUPPORT THE SKY.

In this labour, which took 18,000 years, he was aided by the Four Most Fortunate Beasts who emerged with him from the Egg – the Dragon, the Phoenix, the Unicorn and the Turtle. When the separation was complete, Pangu died. His breath became the wind and clouds, his eyes became the sun and moon. His body became the mountains of the world, watered by his blood, sweat and tears. His hair became the forests, and the fleas on his body became the human race, though some say humans were created later from clay by the goddess Nü wa.

AFTER Pangu's death, the Four Most Fortunate Beasts continued to help the gods and goddesses who appeared in their labour of shaping creation. They also produced others of their own kind. The Phoenix and Unicorn, however, were always rare and have become even more so down the ages; but even today in China people eagerly look out for a Phoenix or Unicorn when a new emperor takes the throne, because their appearance is an omen of blessing on his reign. The Turtle's offspring scattered everywhere but lost much of their divinity in the process, retaining only a spark, which is the reason their shells are used for divination.

Of the four first beasts the Dragon alone multiplied and, according to legend, continued to play an active role on earth. The first dragon is said to have had nine sons whose differing characters are remembered today when their blessings are invoked regarding particular activities with which they are associated. Along with nine phoenixes they also appear in the magnificently bejewelled crowns of the Empresses of China.

Thus we find Pulao carved or cast into the tops of bells and gongs because of his deafening cry when attacked by his arch-enemy the whale; Quiniu carved on the screws and bridges of stringed instruments because of his taste for music; Bixi carved on to stone or jade tablets since he was fond of literature; Baxia, carved at the base of stone pillars and the panniers of pack animals because of his immense strength; Haoxian, carved on the eaves of temples and palaces because of his love of danger; Qiwen carved into the beams of bridges because of his love of water, and on rooftops because he loved to gaze into the distance and is believed to guard against fire; Suanmi carved on the legs of incense burners and the Buddha's throne on account of his calm and peaceful nature; Yazi, carved on sword hilts and blades because of his love of battle; and finally Jiaotu, who is often carved on prison gates because of his passion for argument and habit of resorting to violence.

FROM these nine, they say, are descended most other Chinese dragons, ranging from the celestial ones that support and serve the gods in Heaven down to the crocodiles that inhabit certain marshes and rivers in the south. These are often called dragons by the locals, but they make it clear that they consider them to have no closer relation to true dragons than common turtles have with their divine progenitor. That is to say, there is a certain connection and even some

superstition linking crocodiles with rainmaking, but not enough to stop the people killing and eating the beasts given the chance. Their only reservation comes from knowing the crocodiles would as happily eat *them* given the chance. Crocodile flesh is highly prized, especially at marriage feasts in the south, but the tail is believed poisonous. Drums are made of the skin and used to sound the passing hours of the night watch and in ceremonies encouraging rain.

It seems, though, that when the Chinese first came into conflict with crocodiles in the south, they were not at all sure about their nature, and whether they could be killed without incurring the wrath of weather-making dragons. While visiting the Chaozhou district of Guangdong province in the south we were shown a document that showed the matter had been seriously discussed at the very highest levels. It was a proclamation by the local governor Han Yu, dated the 14th year of the reign of Emperor Yuandi (48 – 33 BC), addressed to the crocodiles that then terrorized the rivers and swamps of the district, devouring humans and livestock alike.

After goat and cattle carcasses had been thrown into the water to attract the crocodiles' attention, the governor addressed them at some length, declaring his authority under the Son

of Heaven, the reigning emperor, and his grievances against the beasts. Finally the crocodiles were given an ultimatum, to remove themselves further towards the coast.

First they were given three days to go; but, declared the governor, if they did not go in three days he would be tolerant and give them five. And if they were not gone in five days, he would give them seven. But if they had not moved away by then, they would become lawful prey for hunters. For if they did not leave, said the governor, it proved that they were either in defiance of the divinely appointed Emperor, whose authority derived from the Dragon Emperor himself, or else that they were dumb beasts incapable of understanding a word he was saying. Either way they became fair game for hunters. Thus, after the crocodiles had carefully been given every chance to prove themselves true dragons, they were deemed mere animals that anyone was entitled to hunt.

Between the two extremes of the celestial dragon and the crocodile we have horned dragons, winged dragons, wingless dragons, coiling dragons and many other varieties that we will attempt to outline later.

For many years after the Creation there was peace and harmony between all the entities that came into being. Then war broke out between the gods during which the sky was shattered and everything thrown into confusion. This damage was put right by the goddess Nü wa. As an ancient book called the *Liezi* describes it:

In ancient times the four cardinal points were out of alignment, the Nine Provinces lay open, the sky did not wholly cover the earth and the earth did not wholly support the sky. Fire burned ceaselessly without dying out, the waters flowed endlessly, wild beasts devoured the peaceful people and birds of prey carried off children and the old. Then Nü wa smelted the stones of five colours and repaired the azure sky. She cut off the feet of the tortoise to fix the cardinal points. She slew the black dragon that ravaged the country of Qi. She piled up reeds to quell the overflowing waters. Then all became tranquil and the universe was again at peace.

There followed a golden age of such fruitfulness that humans had only to wander through the fields to find all they needed to eat. Children could safely play with tigers and bears. Nü wa and her consort Fuxi are often called the parents of the human race. Some say Nü wa created them in the first place from clay, but whether or not this was so, all agree that she and her husband were parents in the sense that they first taught them the elements of civilization and order. Nü wa is said to have taught the first humans many domestic arts and to have created the institution of marriage to stabilize family relationships. Fuxi presented to them many

CHINESE UNICORN OR QI LIN, HERALD OF GOOD FORTUNE. NEW—BORN BABIES OFTEN HAVE PICTURES OF IT PINNED TO THEIR COTS TO ATTRACT THE CREATURE'S BLESSING.

skills, including the kindling of fire, making fishing nets and music. Most profound of all was his gift of the eight trigrams, symbols made of three broken or unbroken lines, which formed the basis of writing and divination. These he received from the Yellow Dragon who rose out of a river in the form of a dragon horse, or unicorn, with the symbols inscribed on its back.

NÜ WA and Fuxi are often shown as humans down to the waist and dragons below, because it was in the form of dragons that they carved out the rivers of the world and drained the floods. When their work was complete, they rode off to Heaven in a thunder cart drawn by one winged dragon and two green dragons; a white dragon led the way and a winged serpent followed behind.

There followed other upheavals and wars between the gods, but peace was finally established again under the Yellow Emperor Huangdi, the first of the five legendary emperors who preceded the established dynasties of China. The home of the gods on earth at this time was on the summit of Mount Kunlun at the centre of the world. This was said to lie far to the west in China, on the northern edge of the Tibetan Plateau.

THE DIVINE YELLOW EMPEROR HUANGDI WHO RULED THE EARTH FROM HIS PALACE ON MT KUNLUN AND TAUGHT MANY OF THE ARTS OF CIVILIZATION TO THE ANCESTORS OF THE CHINESE.

This palace was built entirely of jade and contained five cities, one at the centre surrounded by four others. Around them all were ranged twelve towers with nine gates between them on each side. Nine rings of smaller mountains surrounded Kunlun like city walls. Beyond them was a monster-haunted abyss containing the Ruoshi River whose crimson waters were so 'weak' that not even a feather would float upon them. Hence it was often said that the only way for a mortal to reach Mount Kunlun was riding on the back of a dragon. Beyond the abyss was a ring of fiery mountains which burned day and night, lighting the clouds and the cliffs of Kunlun.

To the north-east on the Jade Mountain, Huaijiang, was the Hanging Peach Garden from which a ladder rose to Heaven and which the Yellow Emperor often visited to refresh his spirits. This garden was tended by Xiwangmu, the Queen Mother of the West, a beautiful but often wild and capricious goddess. Her garden contained certain everlasting peach trees which bloomed only once every 3,000 years and gave fruit (Pan Tao) only after another 3,000. When this happened Xiwangmu held a great feast to celebrate her birthday. It was attended by all the Immortals who came to drink of an elixir she made from the magical peaches that renewed their immortality.

From his palace on Kunlun the divine Yellow Emperor, Huangdi, surveyed and ruled the world, assigning lesser emperors to govern the Four Quarters and their corresponding elements

XIWANGMU, THE LEGENDARY QUEEN MOTHER OF THE WEST WHO TENDED THE SACRED TREES ON MT KUNLUN WHOSE PEACHES GRANT IMMORTALITY.

and seasons. Like Fuxi and Nü wa he taught humans the arts of civilization and chief of his gifts was a treatise on medicine, said to have formed the basis of all later Chinese medicine. Among its revelations was the recipe for making a pill that granted immortality and the secret of making gold from base metals. These alchemical secrets were lost and many a later emperor has launched wide but fruitless searches for them in the archives. Huangdi's wife Lei Zu is said to have shown humans how to make silk from the cocoons of silkworms.

'SUDDENLY OUT OF THE CLOUDS CAME A GREAT GOLDEN DRAGON WHO FLEW THE YELLOW EMPEROR AND SEVENTY OTHER GODS TO HEAVEN ON HIS BACK.'

Among those left behind was Ying Long, the Winged Dragon, despite his heroic service in the wars. He moved to Mount Xiongli in the far south and lived there in mountain pools, bringing rain to the people when there was drought. He remained one of the mightiest dragons on earth and helped restore the world again after the Great Deluge that occurred later, during the reign of the Emperor Yao, fourth in succession from Huangdi. This appears to be the same Deluge that we read of in the Bible and Ying Long was Yao's main helper in recreating the rivers of

FINALLY, to commemorate his establishment of order in the world, Huangdi ordered the casting of a great three-legged bronze cauldron engraved with flying dragons, gods, demons and all manner of animals – a vision of creation. This was displayed at a great gathering of gods and earthly princes on the mountain Jingshan. Suddenly out of the clouds came a great golden dragon who flew the Yellow Emperor and seventy other gods to Heaven on his back, after which the palace on Mt Kunlun fell into decay or was itself transferred to Heaven. From Heaven Huangdi continued to keep an eye on the world for a time, but then gradually handed control to the August Personage of Jade who will himself in time be succeeded by another.

China and thus helping to drain the flood, but he appears to have held no special place in the dragon empire.

Other disasters besides the Flood threatened the world during Yao's reign. The most celebrated of these is the rebellion of the ten suns. At this time, it is said there used to be ten suns and twelve moons, which took turns to travel across the sky and bring light to the world. Each morning the ten suns would be bathed by their mother in a pool at the eastern edge of the world, in a place known as the Valley of Light on the mountain Tai Shan in Shandong province, a place of pilgrimage to this day. Above the pool rose a vast mulberry tree, Fo Sang. After bathing,

'ALL TEN SUNS ROSE INTO THE SKY AT ONCE.'

the shining suns would mount into the tree and rest in the lower branches; all save one who climbed to the top where waited a chariot drawn by dragons to bear him across the heavens to Mount Yenzi in the far west. There was a tree here too with glowing crimson flowers where the sun dismounted and climbed down to the lake below, by means of which he returned to the Valley of Light in the east.

When, towards the end of Yao's reign, a dispute arose over his successor, all ten suns rose into the sky at once. The world would have been scorched to a cinder were it not for the Excellent Archer, Yi, who shot nine of them out of the sky, leaving just the one who has lit the day ever since. Yi now dwells in a palace on the sun, apart from twice a month when he visits his wife Chang'e on the moon.

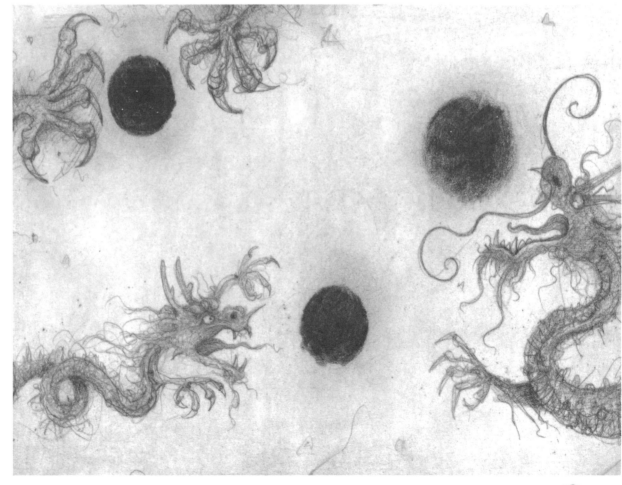

the likeness of nine other beasts. It has the head of a camel, antlers of a deer, eyes of a demon, ears of a bull, throat of a snake, paws of a tiger, claws of an eagle and the scales of a carp. These scales number eighty-one, this being nine (which is the number of a dragon) multiplied by itself and hence the luckiest of numbers. Under its throat the scales are reversed and beneath its chin is a bright pearl, the most fortunate of gems because it is the source of the dragon's power. This pearl has the charm of multiplying anything with which it comes into contact. If placed in a purse of gold, the purse will be overflowing the next morning. If placed in a sack of rice the same will happen.

The voice of the Lung is as the chiming of a gong. Some say the Lung is deaf and that is the meaning of its name, but we have not found this to be so. It is

WITH the departure of most of the gods to Heaven and their increasing remoteness from human affairs, dragons took over many of their duties, particularly those regulating the weather and waters of the world. They established an empire of their own, modelled on that of the gods. They also helped establish the Chinese Empire.

Among the many varieties of dragon listed by the Chinese, the most common and powerful are those with horns, which are generally called Lung or Long. A passage by the sage Wang Fu, which we found in an old book, says of the horned dragon:

The Lung lives in the sky during summer and hibernates in deep pools during winter. It has

YEAR OF THE DRAGON

true that the Lung has no ears but it gathers sound through its two horns. On each side of its mouth are whiskers and on top of the head the Poh Shan, the wooden foot-rule without which it cannot fly to Heaven. When its breath escapes it forms clouds, sometimes becoming rain and sometimes changing to fire. When dragon breath meets dampness it becomes bright. When meeting water it becomes flame. This dragon flame can be extinguished by ordinary fire. The dragon is fond of roasted swallows, which should be offered in sacrifice when rain is needed. It is also fond of arsenic. It fears the centipede (see text 1, right) leaves of the lien tree (Melia azedarach, the blue-flowered Bead or Chinaberry tree), and silk thread dyed with the five sacred colours. It is also afraid of iron because one of the few ways to kill a dragon is with an iron needle or lance.

CHINESE Dragons are said to have the eyes of demons because they are fiery, mesmerizing, and other-worldly. The dragon is easily able to paralyse the human will by its gaze, like the gorgons of Greek myth who turned men to stone. For this reason fierce dragons' heads are often positioned to warn off possible wrongdoers in temples, treasuries and other such places that attract robbers. They are a reminder that human justice might be fallible, but divine retribution is inescapable. They are also there to frighten away demons that might be tempted to enter. Fierce dragon's heads are also often fashioned into door-knockers and the handles of treasure chests for the same reason.

1. DRAGONS ARE AFRAID OF CENTIPEDES, IT SEEMS, BECAUSE GIVEN THE CHANCE THEY CRAWL UP THE DRAGON'S NOSE AND FEAST UPON ITS BRAIN. BLACK DRAGONS ARE ALSO AFRAID OF TIGERS, PARTICULARLY WHITE TIGERS, BECAUSE THEY ARE STRONGER. OTHER DRAGONS ARE LESS FEARFUL, BUT IT IS SAID THAT WHEN A DRAGON AND TIGER MEET, THEY WILL ALWAYS FIGHT.

THE Poh Shan or 'wooden foot-rule' on the dragon's head is a mysterious attribute but is mentioned so often in descriptions of dragons that it cannot be ignored. A dragon is said to be unable to ascend to Heaven without it but nowhere could we learn the reason for how the beast acquires the object and what exactly its function is. There are suggestions that the dragon in fact breathes through it, but again we could learn no reason why it should have to do this in order to fly.

The true dragon, it is often said, never shows itself to mortals all at once. It is always wreathed in clouds and so will show just its head, tail or a portion of its body at any one time. Despite this we found many Chinese who swore that they have seen dragons with their own eyes and are as certain of it as they are of seeing oxen in the fields. In particular we met many sailors on the South China Sea who claimed to have seen dragons clearly ascending to Heaven in waterspouts.

There are said to be four principal types of Lung: Celestial Dragons (Tienlong), who protect and support the mansions of the gods and draw their chariots; Spiritual Dragons (Shenlong) who govern the wind and rains; Earth Dragons (Dilong)

who preside over rivers and streams; and the Dragons of Hidden Treasures (Fucanglong) who guard buried treasure, both natural and man-made. The Dragons of Hidden Treasure are also said to be responsible for volcanoes and produce gaping, lava-filled fissures in the ground when they leave their lairs to visit Heaven. Of these four the Shenlong or Spiritual Dragon is the most celebrated in art and legend, though some say that he is just the male counterpart of the Earth Dragon who flies only in order to mate.

In the watery depths during winter Spiritual Dragons are said to live in crystal palaces piled with gems, pearls and other precious things that the currents have washed down to them. They control the weather

and the waters of the world. They can cause drought and flood and sweet, beneficent rain that makes the crops burgeon. Mostly they are benevolent but they are also proud and volatile creatures. If neglected by humans, they in turn neglect to mind the weather so that drought or flood often follows until they are calmed in some way. This is the origin of the dragonboat races held in many parts of China, at the summer solstice particularly. These sports are designed to entertain and flatter the Lung and so ensure his blessing on the crops.

Most dragons are viewed as benevolent, god-like beings, but some have been feared for their wild and unpredictable ways. The most famous we heard of was the Red Dragon of the South, Qiantang, who caused such devastating floods with his wild temper that Shangdi, supreme ruler of Heaven, sentenced him to be shackled to a pillar in the dungeons of his own brother's underwater palace,

and there he remained for 2,000 years until he won his freedom. How this happened is the subject of a popular tale we heard in many different parts of China. It tells of a student called Liu Ye who failed his exams and had to go home in disgrace.

On his way he bumped into a beautiful girl sadly tending goats by the River Qing. So sad did she seem that Liu Ye forgot his own troubles and asked what the matter was. The girl told him she was a princess who had been tricked into marriage by a tyrant who had cut her off from her family and made her work as a slave while he idled in luxury on her dowry.

She begged Liu Ye to take a message to her father and

'IN THE WATERY DEPTHS DURING WINTER, DRAGONS ARE SAID TO LIVE IN CRYSTAL PALACES PILED WITH GEMS, PEARLS AND OTHER PRECIOUS THINGS THAT THE CURRENTS HAVE WASHED DOWN TO THEM.'

he of course agreed, being already more than half in love with her. Following her directions, he travelled to Dongting lake, famous for its shrimps, and waited by a pine tree which the girl had described to him. Sure enough, there soon appeared as if from nowhere a palace guard who came and asked the student his business there. He explained that he had a letter for the girl's father and the guard agreed to take him if he promised to close his eyes until told to look again. Liu Ye agreed and there followed a strange journey filled with the sound of water. Despite temptation, the student kept to his word and when finally he was allowed to look he found himself in a marvellous underwater crystal palace heaped with piles of gems and other treasures. Two lines of courtiers wearing the richest of silk robes led to a magnificent throne on which sat a handsome man with a flowing green beard, wearing purple who was toying with a jade tablet.

Now although everyone there had human form, Liu Ye immediately knew he was in the court of a dragon king and was terrified but, remembering his charge, he approached the throne and handed over the letter. The king read it aloud and there was fury and grief in the palace when they learned of the cruel fate that had befallen their beloved princess. This din carried to where the wild dragon Qiantang was chained in the dungeons below, and he was moved to such rage on his niece's behalf that he snapped the pillar to which he was shackled and exploded through the palace like a thunderstorm, crimson fire streaming from his eyes and the broken pillar trailing behind him like a reed.

In what seemed next to no time Qiantang was back, in human form and with the princess by his side.

PINE TREES ARE HELD IN SPECIAL REVERENCE BY THE CHINESE. SINCE THEY CAN SURVIVE IN HARSH CLIMATES AND NEVER LOSE THEIR NEEDLES, THEY ARE USED AS SYMBOLS OF LONGEVITY IN POETRY AND ART. AN ANCIENT PINE ON TAI SHANG, THE SACRED MOUNTAIN OF THE EAST, WAS GIVEN THE RANK OF MANDARIN OF THE FIFTH CLASS BY THE FIRST EMPEROR OF THE QIN DYNASTY.

WOODEN DOLL OF A PRINCESS PREPARING FOR MARRIAGE

He had, he proudly declared, eaten the girl's wretched husband, the son of the dragon king of the Qing River. He had also, incidentally, caused a flood that had drowned 60,000 people, but for once had been so stricken with remorse that he had gone straight to Heaven to explain himself and submit to whatever punishment the supreme lord of Heaven decreed.

Shangdi had been so impressed by this new humility that he had forgiven the Red Dragon and decided to restore him to his former glory as Dragon Lord of the South. Then, to celebrate the freeing of both the princess and her uncle, a great feast was held for all the dragon lords of lake, river and ocean. Liu Ye was naturally invited and in due course he and the princess fell in love, married and Liu was granted all the powers of a dragon prince himself.

THE DRAGON KING OF DONGTING LAKE.

On another occasion Shangdi is said to have sentenced another dragon to death by beheading for causing floods. The Chinese Emperor Taizong (AD 627 – 650) himself pleaded for clemency on the dragon's behalf, but was overruled by the heavenly court. Later, when Taizong fell ill and was plagued by nightmares, he believed he was being haunted by the ghost of the beheaded dragon for not trying harder. Two heroes offered to guard the bedchamber doors and succeeded in keeping the demon at bay for a while until it found another way in. So that way, too, was guarded by a hero and so on until at last the Emperor's nightmares ceased altogether. After a while just the figures of the heroes were painted on the doors and still the demon was kept at bay. And this, they say, is the origin of the heavily armed warriors or Men Shen painted on so many doors in China, and which are ceremonially repainted each New Year.

THE DRAGON EMPIRE

THE ORGANIZATION OF THE CHINESE EMPIRE, WITH ITS INTRICATE HIERARCHY AND ITS ENDLESSLY SUBDIVIDED MINISTRIES, IS SAID TO BE MODELLED ON THAT OF THE DRAGONS' OWN EMPIRE, WHICH IS ITSELF DERIVED FROM THAT OF THE SUPREME BEING IN HEAVEN. SO THE DRAGONS TOO HAVE A YELLOW EMPEROR WHO LIVES IN A HEAVENLY PALACE WITH THE AUGUST PERSONAGE OF JADE AND IS ANSWERABLE ONLY TO HIM. HE HAS FIVE CLAWS TO SIGNIFY HIS MASTERY OF THE FIVE DIRECTIONS (THE FOUR CARDINAL POINTS PLUS THE CENTRE).

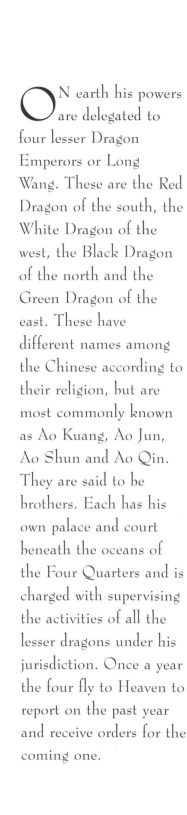

ON earth his powers are delegated to four lesser Dragon Emperors or Long Wang. These are the Red Dragon of the south, the White Dragon of the west, the Black Dragon of the north and the Green Dragon of the east. These have different names among the Chinese according to their religion, but are most commonly known as Ao Kuang, Ao Jun, Ao Shun and Ao Qin. They are said to be brothers. Each has his own palace and court beneath the oceans of the Four Quarters and is charged with supervising the activities of all the lesser dragons under his jurisdiction. Once a year the four fly to Heaven to report on the past year and receive orders for the coming one.

THE Yellow Dragon also has countless other ministers within his own imperial court, each of whom oversees a certain department and can, if necessary, overrule the decrees of any of the Emperors of the Four Quarters. Chief of these ministries is the Treasury of Waters (Shui Fu). This department itself is said to have a Supreme Council and many lesser branches such as the General Department of Salt Waters, the Special Department of Salt Waters and the Department of Sweet Waters. The Governing Council of the Department of Sweet Waters consists of the dragons of the four main rivers of China and the major lakes, plus the Dragons of Indefinite Jurisdiction who have no fixed abode.

APART from sailors and others who make their living from the sea, the ministry of main interest to most Chinese is the Department of Sweet Waters, because their welfare is so dependent on the right measure of rain. They have countless ways of engaging the goodwill of the dragons believed responsible for rain, or even at times forcing their co-operation.

When making their offerings people generally burn incense to attract the dragon's attention and into the glowing brazier they also throw little prayer papers declaring who they are and the specific object of their prayers. The offerings that rich people throw into lakes to please the dragon include gold, silver, precious stones (especially pearls and opals) and

jade, which is held in peculiar reverence among the Chinese. In Heaven there is said to be a particular form of jade that dragons and the gods eat. When crossing rivers rich people also often throw in discs of jade to ensure safe passage, particularly on the Yellow River, known as 'China's Sorrow' because of the frequent devastation caused by its flooding.

OFFERINGS BOWL.

POORER people appeal to the dragon's appetites and offer various foods, including lotus flowers and roasted swallows, of which dragons are said to be inordinately fond. So much so that people are warned against venturing out on the waves after eating roasted swallows because the dragon may smell it, come to the surface for its snack and then grow angry at having been cheated of it. Cream is another favourite delicacy and at many temples you will find bowls of cream left by the water's edge. On the other hand the Mong plant, a favourite human delicacy, only makes dragons irritable and can upset the weather.

Not all dragons are held in equally high regard, however. In many areas people seem less respectful of their local dragons; or perhaps they simply do not believe that theirs is a particularly high-ranking member of the species. When drought comes they will first of all make offerings but then quickly resort to force, riding out on the lake and banging gongs, drums and even pots and pans, anything they can lay their hands on, to wake the beast up and drive it out of the lake and into the clouds to make rain. They even stir the waters with long iron lances because they know the dragon is afraid of iron and steel, and throw in tiger bones to remind them of their ancestral enemies. Besides this they sometimes remove the dragon's statue from the temple and leave it by the side of some dusty road to impress upon it the need for rain. When the rain does come, the statue is borne back into the temple with great ceremony and a festival of rejoicing held, often lasting for days.

At the lake of Kiao Chew we also heard how during one drought, when all the usual means had failed, the people dammed and diverted all streams flowing into it, thus starving the dragon of both fish and fresh water until finally it became so enraged it flew up into the sky and the rains came.

So some dragons appear to be less god-like than others, and some are even simply wicked and behave much like the dragons in our legends of the West. At a lake called the Azure Dragon Pool, north of the Wutai Hills, the Buddhist monks dwelling nearby say 500 evil dragons have been confined by the dragon lords. Generally they do little harm but every day at noon a thick mist gathers on the lake and fishermen avoid it. Also it is said that if any female goes near the lake a great thunderstorm blows up and the lake belches poisonous fumes that instantly kill her.

IN SPRING THE CHINESE HAVE COUNTLESS WAYS OF COAXING OR FORCING THEIR LOCAL DRAGON OUT OF ITS LAKE OR RIVER AND UP INTO THE CLOUDS TO MAKE RAIN.

At Longyan in Fujian Province we heard of an evil dragon who once inhabited a pool in the mountains nearby. Local people soon learned to avoid the place but a party of travelling merchants happened to rest there without having been warned. They were killed and eaten by the dragon and when a priest, Pan To, heard this he decided it was time that something was done. So he went to the kingdom of Wuchang where for four long years he

studied the secrets of dragons. Then he returned to the pool, summoned the dragon by force and led him off to another lake in the west where the Dragon Prince of Wuchang dwelt and delivered him to justice, after which there was no more trouble.

This Dragon Prince is still honoured by the king of Wuchang who often visits the lake to thank the Prince for his blessings, throwing into it offerings of jade, gold, precious stones, pearls and other valuables. There is a monastery nearby with

'SOME DRAGONS APPEAR TO BE LESS GOD-LIKE THAN OTHERS, AND SOME ARE EVEN SIMPLY WICKED AND BEHAVE MUCH LIKE DRAGONS IN OUR LEGENDS OF THE WEST.'

fifty monks who depend upon the dragon's bounty for their survival, for it is said he throws some of the treasures back to them on the shore, and that is how they support themselves. For this reason it is called the Dragon Prince Monastery.

A travelling merchant from Yunnan Province in the foothills of the Himalayas told us the tale of a peasant and his daughter who lived long ago near Horse Ear Mountain (Mai Shang) in Yunnan, whose twin peaks, they say, exactly resemble their name.

During a great drought the peasant and his daughter took to climbing on to the heights, looking for food and anything else they could sell in the market. One day when her father was ill the girl went alone and found a beautiful clear lake high among the hills. As she rested overlooking the lake she thought how sad it was that so much water

INTERTWINED DRAGONS ON A BUILDING IN YUNNAN.

should be locked up there when it could water all the fields of her village and save her father these climbs into the hills that were proving too much for him. She made a song of these thoughts and a wild goose that was passing by landed and told her

that there was indeed a golden key that could release the waters to flow down into her valley; but that it belonged to the Dragon King of the South who guarded it closely among his treasures. But, the goose continued, if she could befriend the third

daughter of the king, she might get help that way, and that princess loved nothing better than beautiful singing.

Now the peasant girl had no idea where the Dragon King's daughter might be found but she journeyed south, asking along the way and singing all the while, until one day a strange young woman appeared who could not hear enough of her songs. They became friends and it turned out that the stranger was indeed the Dragon King's daughter who had secretly slipped away from her father's palace to learn new songs. The peasant girl told her story and the princess agreed to help her. Together they went to the Dragon King's palace under the sea. They stood outside the treasury and sang together until the guardian came to listen. Then the peasant girl slipped into the

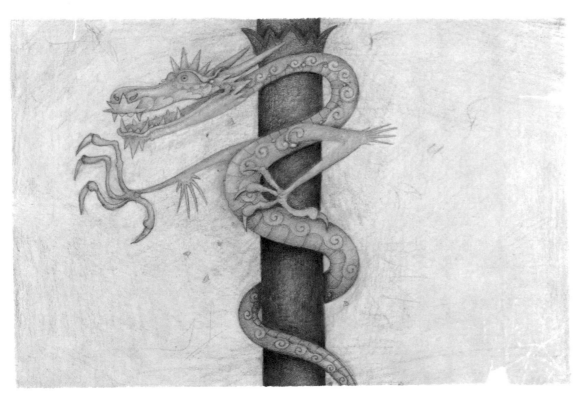

treasury and hunted among the pearls and opals and other precious things until, in a wooden box which she knocked over by accident, she at last found the golden key.

Together they returned to the lake and unlocked the waters to flow down to the valley. Where they threatened to flood, the princess raised fences of straw, which it is said can still be seen today although they have turned to stone, and the drought was lifted. The Dragon King of the South was furious when he learned what had happened, and banned his daughter from ever returning home. But she stayed with her new friend near Horse Ear Mountain where they became famous singers, and their deed is still celebrated today by the local women with a festival of song in the third week of the seventh month.

ENSURING rain is also the chief object of the Dragonboat Festival (Duanwu) held on the fifth day of the fifth lunar month, about the time of the longest day of the year. The main feature of this event is a boat race that is staged on all major Chinese lakes and rivers. Since ancient times this has been held to be one of the most dangerous periods, when the ripening crops are most vulnerable to drought and when pestilence waits to strike man and beast alike. The aim of the Dragonboat Festival is to honour the dragons and by enacting battle between the dragonboats, to stir like thoughts in the divine creatures, because it is the battling of dragons in the sky as well as their mating that brings rain.

The boats are wonderfully lifelike, being narrow canoes up to thirty paces long with the carved head, tail and often the legs of dragons along the sides. They are painted in bright colours, particularly red, because that is the colour of heat and summer. Also it is the colour of the number five, which is the date of the festival. Just before the race there is an elaborate ceremony called 'Awakening the Dragon' where, amidst clouds of incense and a din of musical instruments and detonating firecrackers, the eyes are painted in. This is believed to imbue the vessel and its crew with something of the true dragon's spirit and also calls down the blessing of the Goddess of the Sea. Money and other offerings are also stuffed into the dragonboats' mouths and thrown into the water to appease the true dragons below.

The dragonboats are crammed with oarsmen in pairs, plus drummers at the front and sometimes in the middle to keep time. A helmsman at the rear steers the boat with a long paddle. Vast crowds gather to watch the race, making such a din with their screams and cheering, drums, whistles and firecrackers, that it is easy to imagine oneself on a battlefield. Indeed, the contest between the boats is often as much a battle as it is a race and the spectators often pelt rival boats with rocks and other missiles to try to capsize them, which

often happens. It is considered very lucky if at least one person then drowns, because such people are believed to become messengers for the people, visiting the dragons in person to deliver the prayers of the people and then going straight to Heaven. Indeed it is often said that if at least one person does not drown, drought is sure to follow. In the old days when the rains failed to arrive, brave volunteers would willingly submit to being cast into the waters with heavy weights tied to their ankles.

At Ye on the Yellow River this was a regular practice until the reign of Duke Wen of Wei in the fourth century BC The sacrifices were usually beautiful maidens who were said to become the dragon's brides and live happily in his underwater palace. The custom was ended by an envoy of the Duke, Ximenbao, who doubted that the victims were as willing as everyone liked to believe. Attending one of the sacrifices, he remarked after a while that plainly the dragon had not been satisfied with his gift because there was no sign of rainclouds. Perhaps, he suggested, this was because the maiden had been too unversed in the ways of dragons to convey the people's needs clearly. Then he had his guards seize the priestess presiding over the ceremony, tie stones to her ankles and throw her into the river too. When still no sign of rain showed, several more priestesses went after their mistress, followed by the governor of the district; after which there was a sudden change of heart among all present and the practice of human sacrifice to the river was abandoned forever.

People say the dragonboat races also commemorate the tragic death of the great poet QuYuan, who lived during the famous era of turmoil in China known as the

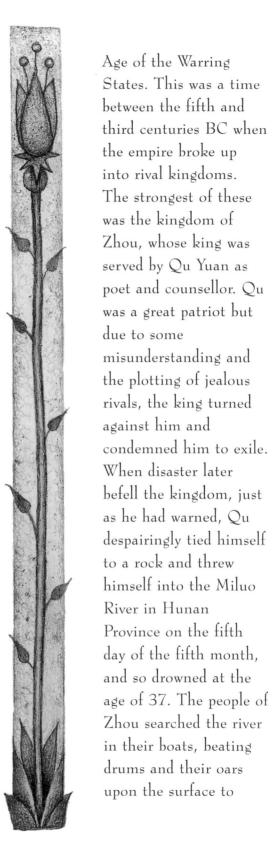

Age of the Warring States. This was a time between the fifth and third centuries BC when the empire broke up into rival kingdoms. The strongest of these was the kingdom of Zhou, whose king was served by Qu Yuan as poet and counsellor. Qu was a great patriot but due to some misunderstanding and the plotting of jealous rivals, the king turned against him and condemned him to exile. When disaster later befell the kingdom, just as he had warned, Qu despairingly tied himself to a rock and threw himself into the Miluo River in Hunan Province on the fifth day of the fifth month, and so drowned at the age of 37. The people of Zhou searched the river in their boats, beating drums and their oars upon the surface to scare away predators. Then in case he still survived in some dragon palace beneath the waves, they cast in rice cakes wrapped in bamboo leaves for him to eat. This is still done today during the dragon races, and rice cakes are a favourite delicacy with the onlookers, stuffed with ham, beans, nuts, eggs and many other delicacies.

Many of Qu Yuan's poems are as famous in China today as in his own time and in one called 'Encountering Sorrow' he describes in allegorical terms (or so one assumes) his search for a new master worthy of his gifts:

2. PENG XIAN WAS A FAMOUS PERFORMER WHO FELL FROM FAVOUR AND DROWNED HIMSELF OUT OF DISAPPOINTMENT.

'Harness winged dragons as my chargers
Build my chariot of ivory and jade
How can I stay with those whose hearts are cold to me?
I leave on a far journey to be rid of them.'
Saying thus, I took the road to Kunlun Mountain,
A long, long way with many a winding turn
The cloud-sewn banner flapped wildly above us
And the jade yoke-bells jangled merrily.

I set off at dawn from the Ford of Heaven
And by evening came to the world's western end.
Phoenixes followed me, bearing my pennants
Soaring high aloft on majestic wings.
'See, I have come to the desert of shifting sands!'
Carefully I steered along the banks of the Red Water
Then, calling the water-dragons to make of themselves a bridge
I summoned the God of the West to take me across.

I tried to curb my mounting steeds and slacken their swift pace
But they soared high up, far into the distance.
We played the Nine Songs and danced the Nine Dances
Snatching time for pleasure and dalliance.
But when we had reached the splendour of the heavens
We suddenly glimpsed below our former home
My groom's heart grew heavy, and our [dragon] steeds for longing
Arched their heads back and refused to go on.

Enough! There are no true men in that land, none to comprehend me
Why should I cleave to the city of my birth?
Since none is worthy of my services in good government
I will go and join Peng Xian [2] in the place where he abides.

BESIDES aiming to avert drought, the Dragonboat Festival is intended to stave off the multitude of pestilences and demons believed to threaten people at this time of year. Children born in the fifth month are said to have difficult natures and houses are scoured and festooned with prophylactic herbs such as calamus, artemesia and garlic. Garlic and other folk remedies such as realgar and cinnabar are added to dishes cooked during the festival. Children and adults also wear tiny and delicately embroidered sachets (Xiang Pao) packed with healing and magical herbs and spices to fend off disease.

The Dragonboat Festival is one of the three great feasts in the Chinese year, all of which are intricately linked with dragons. The others are the Mid Autumn Festival and New Year when great noisy dragon processions are held to remind the hibernating dragons of the coming spring.

The Mid Autumn Festival falls on the fifteenth day of the eighth month in the Chinese calendar, when the moon is full and the days and nights are equal. The date varies by our calendar between September and October because, like our Easter, it is fixed by the phases of the moon rather than the sun. The festival celebrates the harvest and marks the onset of the dry season, when it is believed dragons return from the sky to hibernate in their underwater palaces for the winter. It is more obviously, though, a celebration of the moon, that jewel of the sky so beloved by dragons.

People mark the festival by taking to the hills and parks with lanterns under the full moon to dance, sing, tell tales and perform plays and puppet shows, feasting upon moon cakes filled with lotus and sesame seeds specially baked for the occasion. These contain scraps of paper with wise sayings that are believed to tell the future. They also commemorate the uprising against the Mongol Yuan dynasty in the fourteenth century, which was secretly planned with similar notes hidden in cakes. Women and children make offerings of fruit and cakes to little dolls or paintings of the Hare who is said to live on the moon, where he pounds an elixir of immortality.

The Chinese moon goddess is Chang'e, the wife of Yi, the Excellent Archer who shot down the nine suns when they threatened to scorch the world. The story goes that Yi was once entrusted with some of the elixir of immortality from the Peach Garden of the Queen Mother of the West. He returned home one day to find that his wife had drunk it. He was so furious

that she fled to the moon and asked protection of the Hare who dwelt there. The Hare made peace between them but Chang'e remained on the moon, where Yi built her a palace which he visits twice a month. Although Chang'e is generally portrayed as a beautiful young woman, she is also said to have taken the form of a toad on the moon; which is why common toads are associated with both the moon and long life. Common hares are also linked to the moon by their gestation period, which is exactly one Lunar month.

ALTHOUGH CHANG'E IS GENERALLY PORTRAYED AS A BEAUTIFUL MAID, SHE IS ALSO SAID TO HAVE TAKEN THE FORM OF A TOAD LIVING AMONG THE ROOTS OF THE MAGICAL CINNAMON TREE ON THE MOON. THE BARK OF THIS TREE IS POUNDED BY THE HARE WITH PESTLE AND MORTAR TO MAKE AN ELIXIR OF IMMORTALITY.

THE Chinese New Year Festival begins with the second new moon following the shortest day of the winter, so the date varies between late January and February by our calendar. It is the most important of the Chinese festivals and lasts for over a fortnight. People prepare for weeks beforehand by scrubbing and freshly decorating their houses. On the eve of the event they go around settling debts, making peace with enemies and renewing friendships and family ties. They also make offerings to the household god Zao Guan (Stove Master) because at this time he returns to Heaven for five days to report on their doings over the past year. In particular sticky sweets and honey are offered to sweeten his words or even clamp his jaws altogether. During the rest of the year offerings are also made to his paper image pinned above the stove on the first and fifteenth day of each month, at the new and full moon.

Zao Guan is the most important of the many domestic deities the Chinese believe in (gods of door, window, courtyard, well etc.) because he watches over the household's supply of food. He is said to have once been a human so poor he was forced to sell his wife. Later he worked as a servant for her new husband without realizing it. She took pity and baked him some cakes into which she had hidden money, but he also failed to notice this and sold them for a trifle to a passing stranger. When he learned what he had done he killed himself in despair but Heaven took pity. Instead of becoming a vampirish demon, or gui, the usual fate of suicides, he was made god of the kitchen, because the gods judged that his unfortunate life would incline him to mercy.

THE CHINESE NEW YEAR FESTIVAL BEGINS WITH THE SECOND NEW MOON FOLLOWING THE SHORTEST DAY OF WINTER, WHEN THE MOON RISES JUST BEYOND REACH OF THE DRAGON CONSTELLATION.

THE first day of the New Year is spent with close friends and family. Portraits of the ancestors are brought out of storage and put on display so they can share the feast, and offerings are made before these to secure the intercession of the heavenly powers over the coming year. Then gifts in red wrapping are exchanged between the living and an elaborate meal shared. The second day is spent with more distant relations and the third is called Kai Nian or

'THEN FINALLY THE CELEBRATION IS OVER AND THE ANNUAL ROUND BEGINS AGAIN.'

'Argument Day', because it is believed that if one gets into a dispute on this day, the whole year will be spoiled with arguments. On the fourth day the kitchen god is welcomed back from Heaven and a new image of him and his wife placed above the hearth. The pattern continues until the full moon on the fifteenth day when there begins a three-day carnival with lanterns, fire crackers, drums, music, street theatre and processions of giant paper and silk dragons through the streets, chasing large lanterns representing the sun or moon. Then finally the celebration is over and the annual round begins again.

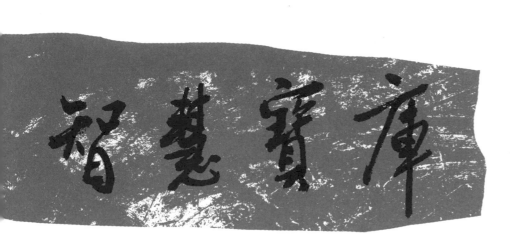

TREASURERS OF WISDOM

OF ALL THE JEWELS THAT GET WASHED DOWN TO THEIR UNDERWATER PALACES, DRAGONS VALUE PEARLS BEYOND ALL ELSE AND FOR THIS REASON THEY ARE A GREAT PERIL TO PEARL-DIVERS, WHOM THEY SEE AS THIEVES. IN CHINA IT IS BELIEVED THAT PEARLS ARE DROPLETS THAT FALL LIKE RAIN FROM THE MOON INTO THE SEA, WHERE THEY ARE OFTEN SWALLOWED BY OYSTERS. SO IT FOLLOWS THAT THE PEARL THAT DRAGONS LONG FOR MOST OF ALL IS THE MOON ITSELF. MANY HAVE BEEN KNOWN TO GO MAD WITH INFATUATION AND TRY TO STEAL IT FROM THE SKY. SO FAR ALL HAVE FAILED, BUT PEOPLE WORRY THAT ONE DAY SOME DRAGON MAY SUCCEED.

THE story of this love has been fixed in the stars with the constellation of the dragon forever chasing the moon across the sky. It is also celebrated in the timing of the Chinese New Year, when the moon rises just beyond reach of the starry dragon, a sign of hope that the mistress of tides and fruitfulness will always escape such rash and consuming lust.

Some dragons are also said to have tried to swallow the sun, but the Chinese say it is always doomed to be burned to a cinder. With the moon there is some doubt, but not with the sun. For this reason many Chinese magistrates

have the figure of a dragon trying to swallow the sun embroidered on their silken robes and wall hangings. It is to declare to the world that it is as impossible for them to be bribed as it is for a dragon to swallow the sun. Whether this is actually true is of course as subject to human vagary as in any other part of the world.

'THE PEARL THAT DRAGONS LONG FOR MOST OF ALL IS THE MOON ITSELF. MANY HAVE BEEN KNOWN TO GO MAD WITH INFATUATION AND TRY TO STEAL IT FROM THE SKY. SOME DRAGONS ARE EVEN SAID TO HAVE TRIED TO SWALLOW THE SUN.'

Besides common pearls and the moon, there are other pearls associated with dragons. One legend says that long, long ago there lived a Jade Dragon in a cave on the east bank of the Celestial River (the Milky Way). In the jungle on the far bank lived a Golden Phoenix and the two were great friends.

JADE DRAGON GUARDING THE MARVELLOUS PEARL.

One day on an island in the river they found a shining pebble and were so enchanted by its beauty that they decided to fashion it into a pearl such as the world had never seen before. So for many months and even years they stayed on the island carefully grinding and polishing the gem and bathing it in the waters of the Celestial River till finally it was a perfect shining sphere, by which time they had grown so close to each other that they remained on the island guarding their treasure.

This pearl was no common gem and the light it gave off was no common light. In the glow of its radiance spring, summer and autumn ruled together all year round on the island. The trees grew tall, the plants lush and the flowers and fruits grew in such abundance that finally the enchanted island caught the attention of the Queen Mother of the West, Xiwangmu. When she learned the cause of the magic her heart filled with longing for the pearl, so one night she sent a servant to steal it while the Jade Dragon and Golden Phoenix were sleeping. Then she hid it away in her innermost treasury behind nine locked doors.

The dragon and phoenix were distraught when they woke to find their treasure gone. Day and night they searched the island, then the river and then the mountains and forests nearby, all to no avail. Then one day they happened to be passing the Queen Mother's palace at Kunlun and saw it filled with a silvery radiance they

'DAY AND NIGHT THEY SEARCHED THE ISLAND, THEN THE RIVER AND THEN THE MOUNTAINS AND FORESTS NEARBY.'

'THE DRAGON IS ALSO OFTEN SAID TO
HAVE A PEARL BENEATH ITS CHIN.'

recognized. The Queen Mother was holding a great feast to celebrate her birthday and on impulse, unable to keep the secret any longer, she had brought out the stolen pearl for her guests to admire. They were all gazing in wonder and admiration when suddenly in burst the Jade Dragon and Golden Phoenix and accused the Queen Mother of having stolen their treasure.

She was furious and ordered her guards to throw them out. In the struggle that followed, the pearl was tossed through a window and began to fall towards the distant earth. The dragon and phoenix chased it through the air but could not catch up till it landed and became a clear green lake. Unable to part with their treasure, the two creatures settled down beside the lake and to this day Jade Dragon Mountain and Golden Phoenix Mountain still guard the lake in the far west of China.

THE dragon is also often said to have a pearl beneath its chin. Some believe this is an egg which the dragon carries this way to keep it safe until it is ready to hatch; but most people hold that it is a unique gem which in some way encapsulates the dragon's immense wisdom. Hence it has magical powers. In Sichuan Province they tell the story of a poor boy called Xiao Sheng who found such a pearl, which must have been dropped by a dragon flying overhead.

This happened long ago during a great drought when the boy first of all found a patch of lush grass that never diminished, no matter how often he cut it to sell in the market as cattle feed. One day it occurred to Xiao Sheng that instead of travelling all the way to the patch each day to cut grass, he could dig it up and replant it at home. So he dug up the turf by the roots and beneath it found a wonderful pearl. Thinking himself doubly lucky, the boy put it in his pocket and went home, where he planted the grass beside the hut he shared with his widowed mother and then hid the pearl in an almost empty rice jar where no burglar would think of looking.

Next morning they woke to find that the grass had withered and died, but the rice jar was brimming over. That was when they realized they had found a dragon's pearl, because it is a virtue of these gems to multiply whatever they are kept with, be it rice, money or the patch of grass where this one had been found.

From that day Xiao Sheng and his mother lacked for nothing, but because they were generous to their neighbours, rumours soon spread as to the source of their new-found prosperity. In time these tales reached the ears of the local landlord who soon turned up with soldiers to demand the pearl, claiming that it must have been found on his property (since he owned all the land in that region) and so rightfully belonged to him.

Rather than hand it over, Xiao Sheng swallowed the pearl. Immediately his stomach felt filled with a raging fire so he ran to the muddy trickle nearby which was all that remained of the drought-stricken river and drank and drank till it seemed he would drain it dry. And as he drank, he grew larger and larger and his form changed until the onlookers saw not a boy but a mighty dragon who finally stopped drinking and turned to look around him with a certain wonder in his eyes. The landlord and his soldiers fled but the dragon flew swiftly after them and unleashed a flood which both drowned them and brought blessed relief to the parched land, so that the paddy fields filled and the river flowed strong and full again.

Finally the dragon that had been Xiao Sheng took sad leave of his mother and swam away down river. To this day that stretch of it is called 'Wang Niang Tan', which means the

'Looking-back-at-mother bends', because the twenty-four snakelike bends in the river are said to have been formed by Xiao Sheng who did just that as he departed.

So the dragon's pearl that appears so commonly in Chinese paintings and embroideries can represent many things. It can be a common sea pearl, a luminous mineral, a dragon's egg, the moon or the sun. It is often depicted as a spinning ball trailing flames – a thunder ball symbolizing the thunder and lightning. Or it contains a spiral, which is also said to represent thunder. Some Chinese philosophers have even gone so far as to say that 'the Dragon is thunder', which makes it a very immediate presence over much of China, where thunderstorms are common.

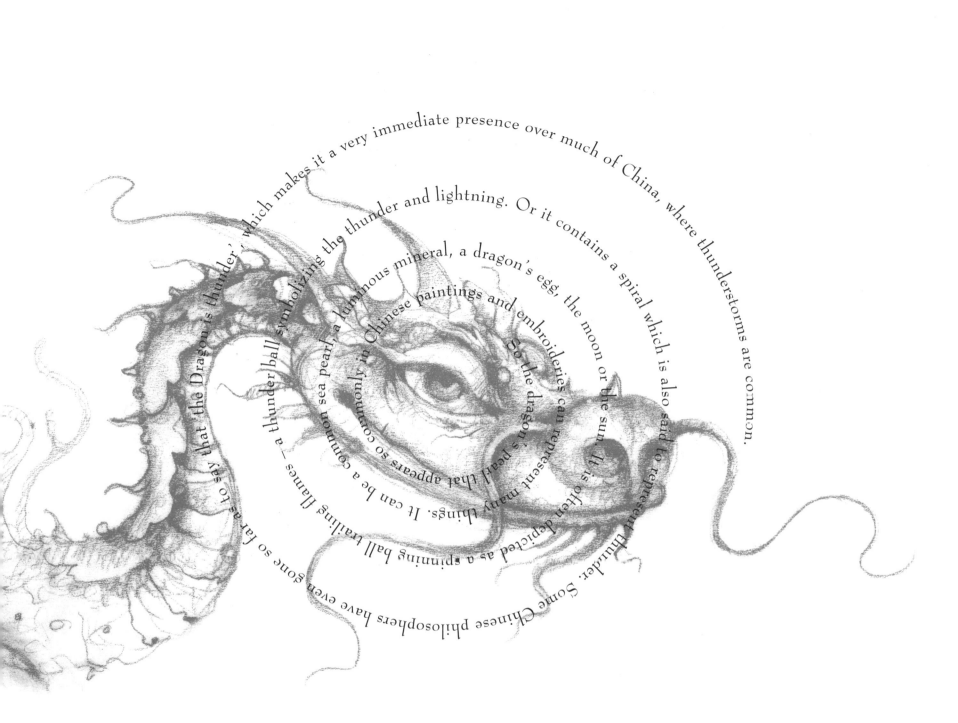

which makes it a very immediate presence over much of China, where thunderstorms are common. Or it contains a spiral which is also said to represent thunder. Some Chinese philosophers have even gone so far as to say that the Dragon is thunder', which symbolizing the thunder and lightning. a thunder ball trailing flames — a common sea pearl, a luminous mineral, a dragon's egg, the moon or the sun. It is often depicted as a spinning ball pearl that appears so commonly in Chinese paintings and embroideries can represent many things. So the dragon's

The dragon's pearl can also stand for something far more subtle – the Yin-Yang disc representing the concept that lies at the heart of all Chinese mysticism and philosophy. This is identical with the Cosmic Egg from which Pangu and the Four Most Favoured Beasts were born at the beginning of creation. In Taoism the dragon is often called the Keeper of the Tao, the greatest and most mysterious treasure of all because the person who possesses it has need of nothing else.

Tao or 'the Way' is, by its very nature, almost impossible to define. Enigmatic riddles and hints can be dropped but they do no more than point towards something that cannot be pinned down in words. Lao Tzu, the founder of Taoism in the sixth century BC, wrote:

> *The way that can be spoken of*
> *Is not the true Way.*
> *The name that can be named*
> *Is not the true Name.*

Confucius is said to have visited Lao Tzu in his youth and on his return told his disciples:

> *I know that a bird flies, a fish swims and a deer runs. For the deer a net can be made, for the fish a line, and for the bird a corded arrow. But the dragon's flight to Heaven on the wind and clouds is something beyond my knowledge. Today I have seen Lao Tzu who is most like a dragon.*

His followers were less impressed by the older man's teachings and there has been rivalry between the two schools of thought ever since. Perhaps this is because Confucianism is an essentially pragmatic philosophy aimed at achieving visible results, while Taoism is a mystical set of teachings aimed at grasping the invisible.

MORE can be said about Yin and Yang, the two constituent elements of Tao. All Chinese philosophy stems from the concept of Yin and Yang, the complementary opposites whose interaction is said to be the seed of all things. Everything, they say, can be measured in terms of its proportion and balance of Yin and Yang. To the Western mind the most curious feature of the concept is that Good and Evil are not among the many dualities listed under each heading. Evil results from an imbalance of Yin and Yang, and Good flows from their harmony, say the Chinese. They are a separate issue and it follows that instead of Evil being seen as a driving, active force to be tackled head on and conquered, as good Christians are taught, it is often viewed as a side issue. Tackle the underlying causes of an evil situation and it will disperse of its own accord, say the Chinese. That at least is the theory. In everyday life people are rarely so detached from their problems.

Most things contain a certain mix of Yin or Yang natural to them, but some tend towards the extremes. These are the qualities generally listed to distinguish them:

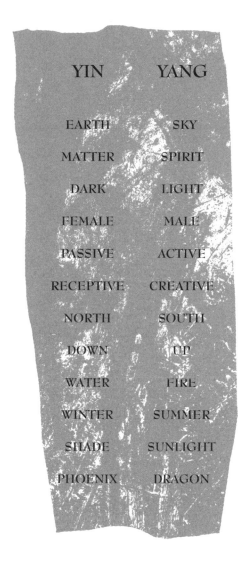

YIN	YANG
EARTH	SKY
MATTER	SPIRIT
DARK	LIGHT
FEMALE	MALE
PASSIVE	ACTIVE
RECEPTIVE	CREATIVE
NORTH	SOUTH
DOWN	UP
WATER	FIRE
WINTER	SUMMER
SHADE	SUNLIGHT
PHOENIX	DRAGON

'IN TAOISM THE DRAGON IS OFTEN CALLED THE KEEPER OF THE TAO.'

The dragon is often called 'the essence of Yang' because its bright, fiery, rainmaking flight to heaven is so clear a picture of the creative principle at work. On this level his Yin counterpart is the phoenix; but as 'Keeper of the Tao' the dragon has his own Yin side, living as he does in the cool, shady depths of water during the winter. Some say the female dragon remains underwater all year, leaving only for aerial mating flights, but the general opinion we found was that both male and female dragons leave the water in spring. It is just custom to call the rainmaking dragon 'he', just as we often refer to cats as 'she'. Perhaps it is their double life that makes the dragon so wise. It understands the interplay of Yin and Yang so well because for half the year it is one, and for half it is the other. This is perhaps the real meaning of the Dragon's Pearl.

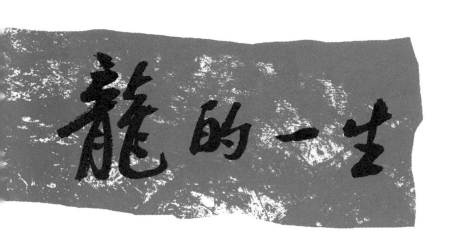

LIFE CYCLE OF DRAGONS

DRAGONS HAVE MANY WAYS OF COMING INTO BEING. MOST ARE BELIEVED TO BE DESCENDED FROM THE ORIGINAL DRAGON THAT APPEARED WHEN PANGU BROKE FREE OF THE COSMIC EGG, BUT THEY HAVE BEEN CREATED IN OTHER WAYS. SOME HAVE SIMPLY COME INTO BEING FULLY FLEDGED, AS IT WERE, LIKE THE GODS THEMSELVES. AS WE HAVE SEEN, SOME HUMANS ARE SAID TO HAVE BECOME DRAGONS FOR ONE REASON OR ANOTHER AND MANY GODS, TOO, SEEM TO ADOPT THE DRAGON FORM AT WILL AND ARE OFTEN PORTRAYED AS HAVING A DRAGON'S OR SERPENT'S BODY WITH A HUMAN HEAD.

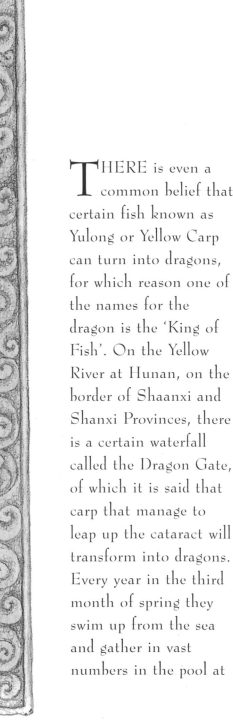

THERE is even a common belief that certain fish known as Yulong or Yellow Carp can turn into dragons, for which reason one of the names for the dragon is the 'King of Fish'. On the Yellow River at Hunan, on the border of Shaanxi and Shanxi Provinces, there is a certain waterfall called the Dragon Gate, of which it is said that carp that manage to leap up the cataract will transform into dragons. Every year in the third month of spring they swim up from the sea and gather in vast numbers in the pool at

the foot of the falls. It is said that only 71 can make the climb in any year. When the first succeeds, then the rains begin to fall. This Dragon Gate is said to have been created after the Flood by the god-emperor Yu who split a

mountain blocking the path of the Yellow River. It is so famous that throughout China you will hear people say that: 'a student facing his examinations is like a carp attempting to leap the Dragon Gate'.

'THERE IS A CERTAIN WATERFALL CALLED THE DRAGON GATE, OF WHICH IT IS SAID THAT CARP THAT MANAGE TO LEAP UP THE CATARACT WILL TRANSFORM INTO DRAGONS.'

HUNAN is not the only place where this happens. Many other waterfalls in China also have the name Dragon Gate and much the same is said about them. Other Dragon Gates we heard of are on the Wei River where it passes through the Qinling Mountains and at Jin in Shanxi Province.

Dragons are, moreover, quite able to adopt other guises by courtesy of which they have interbred with gods, humans and animals. Most commonly, though, dragons are said to arise in the same way as other creatures, from the mating of two other dragons, male and female. When this happens it is a spectacle of terror and wonder to those below. First there comes a rising wind. Then the trees begin to bend and the grass to whisper warnings to take shelter. Then the dragons are heard calling out to each other as they close in across the sky – he descending from above, she rising moist with the scents of field and forest from below. The wind rises further and the clouds build. The world darkens and lightning flashes as the dragons approach each other. The mountains ring with the thunder of their roars and the earth shakes with the clash of their coming together, then bathes in the dragons' bounty as in the joy of their union they open the springs of Heaven to release blessed rain on to the thirsty earth.

Afterwards the female dragon flies away, seeking a place to lay her eggs. This she does with great care because it is not until she carries new life within her that she knows where it should be born. Usually the place she chooses is close to a lake or river, wild and remote from the habitations of men, for the eggs will have to lay there for many hundreds of years before they hatch. Some say it takes

even longer than this. In the western highlands of China, where belief in dragons is very strong, we were assured by a monk that it takes 3,000 years for a dragon's egg to hatch. For the first thousand it lies in a river, for the next thousand its mother transfers it to the mountains and for the final period it is buried close to some river or lake. More commonly, though, it is said that it takes 500 years for the egg to hatch.

Some eggs are said to be large but mostly they are quite small and resemble precious stones of five colours, which grow moist on the surface when rain is coming. We saw several such eggs in a monastery in the Himalayan foothills. They resembled crystalline rocks the size and rough shape of

ostrich eggs, with a small hole from which the dragon was said to have escaped. We were also shown one without a hole within which we could faintly discern what looked like a dragon embryo. The monks told us it had died unborn and they knew this because the egg had lost its power of moistening in advance of rain.

When the eggs hatch, the baby dragons race for the nearest water where, usually over many more hundreds of years, they slowly mature. Although small and weak, these young dragons cannot be harmed without attracting the wrath of their kindred. Often to begin with they have the appearance of white eels, the legs and claws only growing later. At Yan Tang we heard how long ago a man caught what he thought was a white eel in a pool called Smoky Pond. As he was cooking it an old man came by and warned him that it was a young dragon and that disaster would surely follow. And, or so we were told, the man's village was indeed drowned in a flood the next day.

Conversely, we often heard the tale of a hunter called Hai Li Bu who once rescued a white eel from a wild goose. The eel turned out to be a young dragon and Hai Li Bu was rewarded by its mother with the gift of a jewel that enabled him to understand the speech of animals. The only condition was that he was not allowed to reveal what he heard to anyone else or he would turn into stone. For a while Hai Li Bu prospered greatly as a hunter but then one day he overheard from the animals that a great flood was about to drown his village. What to do? In the end he warned the villagers and was turned into a stone that can be seen to this day; but we heard so many different accounts of where it stands that we concluded that it must be a fairytale that the people of many places have adopted as their own.

'IN CERTAIN PARTS OF CHINA WE WERE ASSURED THAT SOME DRAGONS ATTAIN FULL SIZE WITHIN MOMENTS OF HATCHING.'

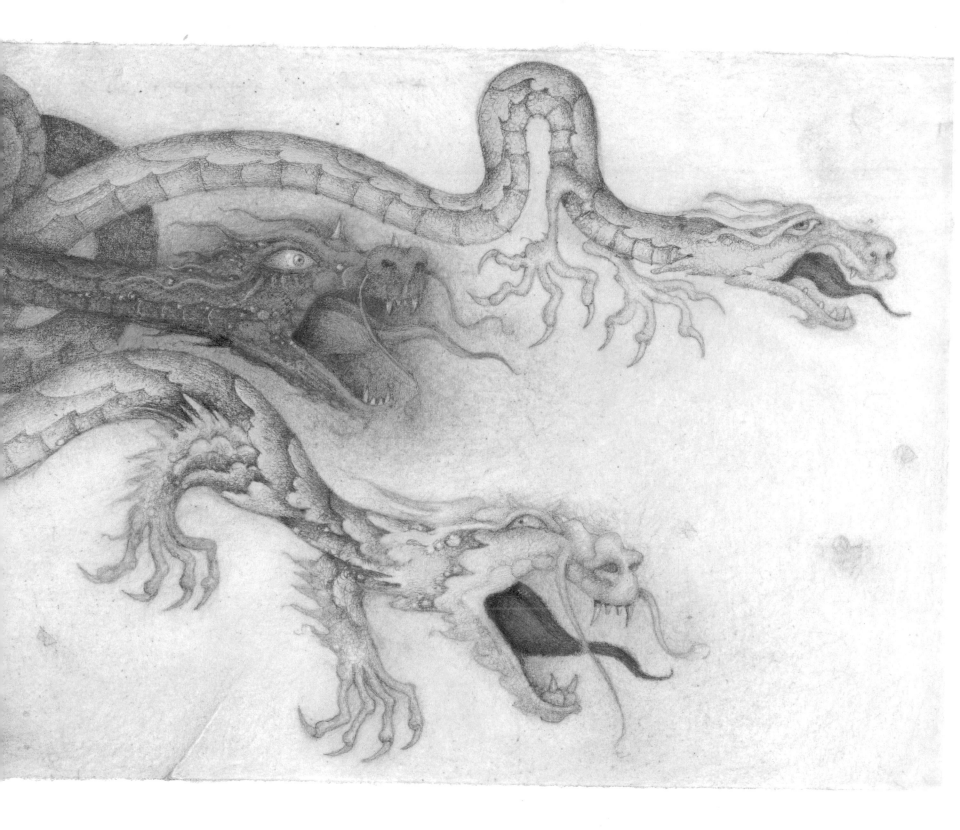

'YOUNG DRAGONS CANNOT BE HARMED WITHOUT ATTRACTING THE WRATH OF THEIR KINDRED.'

The Kiao Lung belongs to the dragon family. Its eyebrows are crossed, hence its name signifies 'the crossed reptile'. It has scales and is more than twelve feet long. It resembles a snake but has four feet and is broad like a shield. It has a small head and a slender neck. The front of its breast is red in colour, its back a variegated green and its sides are patterned. Its tail is composed of fleshy rings and is very powerful. Its eggs are large. It can induce fish to fly but not if a turtle is present. The Emperor Chao of the Han dynasty caught a white Kiao when fishing in the Wei River. It resembled a snake but was without scales. Its head was composed of soft flesh and tusks protruded from its mouth. The Emperor ordered his ministers to cook it and found it delicious. The bones are green and the flesh red.

MOST commonly it is said that for the first 500 years the young dragon resembles a lizard and is called a Pan Long or Coiled Dragon, because it spends much of its time coiled up asleep and building its energies. It is also often called a Kiao Lung, a name that is applied furthermore to certain large lizards or iguanas that inhabit the coasts of southern China and certain isles of the Eastern Ocean. Many people in those parts believe these are true dragons in the first stage of life. An old book we came across in Nanjing says of these creatures:

At 500 years the Coiled Dragon grows horns and hair as soft as that of a calf and of five colours. Over the next 500 years it gradually develops into the Ying Long or True Dragon and becomes ready to ascend to Heaven for the first time. In certain parts of China, though, we were assured that some dragons attain full size within moments of hatching and immediately fly to Heaven in a typhoon, for which reason they consider it very dangerous to keep a dragon's eggs indoors because the building will be destroyed when it hatches.

Either way, when a dragon first rises to Heaven it is a day of wonder because other dragons gather to welcome it and there are violent thunderstorms. A

waterspout rising from a lake is the surest sign that a young dragon is making its first flight, and that the storm is not due to some other cause such as the mating or battling of dragons in the sky.

Many authorities say that until a dragon ascends to Heaven it is a creature of flesh and blood like the ox or turtle and can be killed as easily; but afterwards it becomes a spiritual creature that can adopt any guise it chooses, or even be invisible. Some Chinese dragons are said to have wings but most do not and they are able to fly because of their spiritual nature.

MOST pools and lakes are said to be inhabited by just one dragon at a time, but certain lakes that are home to high-ranking dragons may have several or very many because, like human rulers, they have followers to do their bidding.

Although in Peking you find many people who do not believe dragons exist any longer in the physical sense, they still buy powdered dragon bone or teeth in the local market in total confidence as a potent remedy for many ailments ranging from gout to madness. There is no contradiction in this because they say these bones come from dragons which died long ago.

In certain parts of the country great masses of these bones are found heaped together in the side of landfalls, or the

beds of rivers such as the Tsin in southern Shanxi Province. They are also common in streams running from the caves of the Great Hill (Tai Shan) in Shandong and on the islands of Puning in the Guangdong Province of southern China. East of the Fang Chang hills in the Antui Provence is a plain said to be covered in dragon bones if only one digs down a few feet, and peasants often turn them up with their ox ploughs.

Such places are claimed to be the sites of dragon battles long ago because unless they die in battle or some such

misfortune, dragons are said to live for 10,000 years or even to be immortal. But there is also a common belief that dragons shed their bones every thousand years, just as snakes shed their skin, and visit certain favoured places to do so, which is why the bones are all piled together. In truth it is hard to deny one or other of these explanations. Soon after our first arrival in China we saw many of these bones with our own eyes in Puning before they were broken up for medicine, and it was hard to imagine them coming from any other creature than the dragon. One complete skeleton we witnessed being dug from a hillside was over a hundred feet in length and exactly resembled the impression of dragons we get from Chinese paintings. Whole villages support themselves by digging up these bones and trading them with other parts of the country.

Dragons are also known to slough just their skins from time to time. Then from the scales insects crawl, which turn into red dragonflies known as Dragon's Grandchildren or Dragon's Armour. People fear harming or trapping these insects because it brings illness.

THE pearl beneath a dragon's chin is the most sought after part of its body but very rarely found with buried skeletons. They say it is only found if the beast has died a violent death, and even then only if no other dragon was nearby to remove it. Otherwise, if the dragon is merely moulting its bones, it keeps the pearl itself.

Next in value come dragons' horns, which are held to have a greater virtue as medicine than all the other bones put together. This is because in life the dragon's strength is concentrated in its horns. When ground to powder and mixed with wine, dragon's horn is claimed to remedy falling sickness, stomach cramps, dropsy and

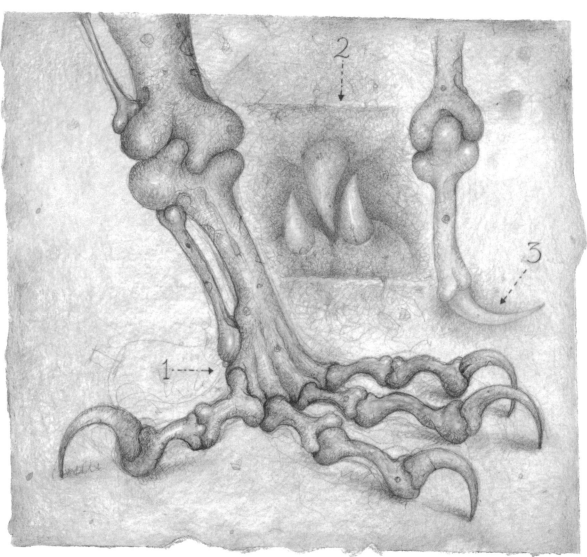

stiffening of the joints. If poured into the eye it will cure cloudiness of vision, though not blurredness. When burned with incense, the smoke of dragon's horn has the virtue of banishing evil spirits from both people and places.

Next in order of importance come the dragon's teeth which, when ground to powder, are said to cure madness and all other upsets of the brain, including headaches. Then come spinal bones and so on down to the toe bones which are the least powerful, though the claws have a similar potency to dragons' teeth. Bones are also graded according to colour, as they come in shades of the five mystic colours of China – red (or pink), green, white, black and yellow. Each is suited to particular ailments usually relating to organs of the body with the same colour. Dragon bone is generally sold in powdered form, but certain variegated bones containing all five colours are sold whole or crushed before the buyer's eyes because these are especially potent and prized almost as much as dragon horn itself. It is said that bones marked with wide lines come from female dragons and those with narrow lines from the male and they are accordingly prescribed for male and female patients.

Dragon spittle is also commonly sold in markets and is said to be found washed up on sea shores. To our eyes it was very similar, maybe identical, to the ambergris we get from sperm whales at home. Besides medicine it is used as a base for the finest perfumes and incense, and an ink applied to jade and gold.

Many other parts of the dragon are offered in the markets but it is widely accepted that most are fakes aimed at the gullible. Only the bones and horns are seriously trusted; and maybe the whiskers which are said to have a charm that attracts fish and repels troublesome insects. The finest whiskers are up to three feet in length and usually deep purple.

Dragon's flesh is said to make the eater more intelligent, but unless one counts the flesh of crocodiles and lizards that are often sold as dragon meat in the markets, this has only ever been put to the test in legend or ancient history. The brain and liver are remedies for dysentery. In the days of the Emperor Wu of the Han dynasty (c. 200 BC – AD 200) it is mentioned in the state chronicles that a dragon once fell from the sky into the palace grounds during a storm and was killed. Upon eating the flesh the Emperor was so pleased by the enhancement of his mental faculties that he ordered a great stew made of it for the improvement of all his chief ministers.

ANCIENT records also show that many emperors have had official Dragon Keepers on their payroll to tend their tame dragons. In latter times the term seems to have been used loosely to cover crocodiles and large lizards kept in the Imperial Zoo, which contains strange and wonderful creatures from around the world, including giraffes from Africa and rhinos from India. But if the legends are taken at face value they were originally employed to care for true dragons, whose welfare was bound up with that of the state.

The custom is said to have been initiated by King Shun of the Xia Dynasty, whose men dug a pair of hairy dragons from their underground lair in the state of Nanxun. The habit was continued by his successors, even Kong Jia who was in most other respects a weak, careless and decadent ruler who let the realm fall apart while he indulged in orgies. This carelessness was in the end his undoing and proved the wisdom of his forefathers in seeing to it that the dragons were properly cared for.

What happened was this: Kong Jia was fond of his dragons but appointed as their Dragon Keeper a shiftless flatterer who knew nothing about dragons but much about charming vain rulers and merely wanted a place amid the glamour of court. The female dragon soon died of neglect and the keeper managed to keep it from the king for a while. Then inevitably the truth came out and he had to make a hasty escape. The king advertized for a new keeper and one presented himself who was almost the opposite of his predecessor. His name was Shih Meng and he knew everything about dragons and nothing about kings. Shih Meng was said to have fairy powers and eat nothing but plum and peach flowers.

Soon he had the king's remaining dragon dancing through the sky like a swallow and glowing with

health. The king was delighted and for a while all went well. Then one day as he was watching the dragon perform, Kong Jia suggested that perhaps the sky dance could be improved by tying golden streamers to the dragon's tail. If he had been more of a diplomat the new Dragon Keeper might have gently talked the king out of the idea, but instead he simply laughed at its silliness and refused to demean the dragon in such a way.

Kong Jia was outraged and threatened to have the Dragon Keeper's head chopped off if he would not obey. Shih Meng seemed strangely unafraid. He refused again and warned the king he would regret it if he carried out the threat. This was again not the most diplomatic thing to say because the king promptly did have his head cut off.

Even though he was dead, people were still rather afraid of Shih Meng, so he was buried far away from the palace in the wilderness. Soon a great storm blew up. Thunder shook the mountains and lightning set the forests ablaze. Seeing a wall of flame advancing on his palace, the king took sudden fright and decided to make amends with the dead Dragon Keeper. So he took offerings to the grave and bowed his head in repentance. Finally the flames died down and the king clambered back into his carriage. But by the time it returned to the palace he too was mysteriously dead.

ONE way or another, dragons played a vigorous part in the fortunes of the First Dynasty of China, the Xia Dynasty that had been founded by Yu, whom legend says was born a dragon. A couple of generations after Kong Jia's strange death he was succeeded by Qie, whose decadence far exceeded anything that had gone before. Qie and his court did nothing but feast in idleness and luxury in the Royal Gardens while the realm fell into chaos and ruin. The pools of the garden, it is said, were filled with wine and the trees hung with every sweetmeat it is possible to imagine, while orchestras played and entertainers danced and juggled.

Often the king did not emerge for months at a time and it is said he had a favourite concubine who could transform herself into a dragon whenever she chose. Her name was Kiao Ki and she was supposed to be able to read the future, but only after she had feasted on human flesh. This outrage is what made the people finally rebel and look to the neighbouring King Tang for deliverance. He marched against Qie, destroyed him and established the Shang Dynasty, which received the blessing of the Dragon Empire and all Heaven.